CORPORATE CROSSOVERS

Praise for working with Wendy Kerr

"I consulted Wendy because I felt helpless and "stuck" in my present situation. Wendy was all about moving forward. Our sessions were professional, logical, focused and well-organised. Wendy's objectivity and experience opened doors and showed me options I never knew existed. I would highly recommend Wendy to anyone with a goal or a dream that seems too overwhelming to achieve." *– Emily Dixon, Tokyo*

"I now have a compelling vision of my future that 12 weeks previous, I would not have dared pursue. With Wendy's help I was able to put together a realistic path to that compelling future. Now I have a plan that bridges the future to the present and the confidence to carry it out. Aside from the intangible benefits of confidence and emotional congruency, there were also very real tangible benefits. I was able to chop two hours off my work day and double my revenue in twelve weeks." *– C. D, Tokyo*

"Since working with Wendy I have resigned my job and I am now working fulltime for myself. The impact has been enormous. It's given me a massive amount of confidence. It has allowed me to focus and to discover that I am actually capable of doing a lot more than I thought. It has allowed me to realise that I actually am a business woman and not someone who has a hobby that is a business." *– Darryn de la Soul, Soul Sound, UK www.soulsound.co.uk*

"I left my corporate environment close to a year ago and I'm in business planning stage, so working with Wendy was perfect for me. It got me thinking about my vision, solidifying it and giving me clarity around where I wanted to go. The best thing about the programme was discovering what made me passionate. It really took my business planning to another level. It was a very focused and very results driven programme. I would highly recommend her to anybody who's looking at starting up their business or who is in their business already." –

Sonya Morton-Firth, Ilu Fitwear, London www.ilufitwear.com

"Wendy has been a really motivational and challenging coach. She's helped me think through fundamental issues for me and come up with a super plan for an exciting future. Coaching helped me to understand creative ways to work with my own clients. Wendy's great fun to work with, but still gets results. The perfect combination...I highly recommend her!" *– J.M, London*

"Wendy has given me confidence to face and analyse where I am, what interests me, what drains me and where my motivation lies. I now have clarity and a less fearful pathway to the vision for my business." *– Sue Chadwick, UK/Zimbabwe Sue Chadwick Jewellery* www.suechadwick.co.uk

"Wendy creates an energised yet safe atmosphere where your wildest career hopes and dreams can be given a voice, and where you leave enthusiastic to take the next step. A positive and affirmative experience." *– Kathleen Drum, London*

"Wendy helped me to get in touch with the passion I feel and how to take it forward to the next stage in my life." *– J. Nathan, London*

"It was inspiring and practical to work with Wendy. I was able to critically look at and get a fresh perspective on my career and aspirations. Now I have an action plan and the motivation to do something about it!" *– Angela Bevington, London*

"Wendy's coaching style combines perfectly the objective, straightforward business advice with the personal, human touch she brings in to help people embrace change with enthusiasm and turn what seems to be insurmountable obstacles into great opportunities. I fully recommend Wendy!" *– Oana Chifu – Romania*

CORPORATE CROSSOVERS

WHEN IT'S TIME TO LEAVE THE OFFICE AND START YOUR OWN BUSINESS

WENDY KERR

Contents

Introduction

So you are fed up with your job...

Imagine if you could do work on your terms, in your way.

Imagine if you had the freedom, flexibility and control to do what you wanted, when you wanted and you felt confident that the money was handled.

- What would you do then?
- How would that transform the way you think about work?
- If work was a place where you created, were appreciated, your voice was heard and you got recognised and rewarded based on your contribution, wouldn't that be worth getting up for?
- What would you create for YOUR new paradigm of work?
- What would you do?
- What would you want to do?

Not what you feel you 'should' do or what will fit in. Just what you actually WANT to do.

Take the time to dream. To imagine.

Not just what you would do but the life you have wanted to create. Capture the dream, the visions you once held that inspired you that set you on a path that, for whatever reason, is now hidden from view.

It's time to embark on a new journey. A quest to live your best life, a quest to create a business that enables you to live the life you desire.

You work to live, not live to work.

I want you to give yourself the permission to do this. I will guide you on your journey, helping you see what's possible, giving you the framework and tools to make it happen. If you decide to, you can have a different life, and work in the way that works for you.

You have been successful in your career so far, and you may be fearful of leaving this to work in a new way. I will bridge that gap by giving you the structure and process to create a business that allows you to live the life you love. You will be walking towards a life that works for you, and be connected with a community of women on a journey just like yours.

> You could switch from your corporate job to running your own business. You could be a Corporate Crossover®.

I'm a Corporate Crossover® and I'm passionate about changing the way work works. I am on a mission to fuel 10,000 women to create a business that allows them to live the life they love.

I left my corporate career to create a successful six-figure coaching and consulting business, running it from Tokyo and London. I work with leaders of high growth, global technology companies in challenging times of expansion and change. My client companies include Expedia, IBM, ACCA, The Economist and Betfair.

Wanting to change the way work works, I have also coached, mentored and fueled over 1,500 women to create a business that allows them to live the life they love.

I've experienced all the struggles and challenges of business ownership and I love to enable women (wherever they are in their journey of leaving their job) to start their business successfully, by providing them with structure, tools, processes and one on one mentoring.

Introduction

Whether you are considering making the leap into self-employment, or you're running your own business and finding it a struggle, this book will help you to set your goals and pursue them.

I will divulge all the push factors that make you want to leave the corporate workplace:

- The toxic environment
- The lack of freedom
- The frustration

And I'll be talking about the pull factors that make you want to be your own boss:

- Making the rules for yourself
- A flexible schedule
- Freedom to do what you want with your time
- Focusing only on the work you enjoy
- Being responsible for all the decisions
- Sidestepping the red tape and unnecessary meetings

But it's not all decision-making and telecommuting from tropical islands, I'm afraid. I'll also cover how to get through the hard times with your business:

- Trying to do it all
- Making less money than you used to
- Limited financial stability
- Working harder than you've ever worked before
- Feeling isolated
- Wondering if it's all worth it

How to use this book

I would love you to think of this book as your travel guide to your new life. To enable you to design how work will work for you from now on. I will start at the start, the thinking of leaving, all the way to the destination of beginning your new business.

I'll take you through those factors that make you want to leave your job, as well as those that make you feel you should stay. I will also look at the emotional journey of your transition and give you the framework and tools to make this as smooth as possible.

To fuel your journey there are lots of exercises, worksheets and tools for you to work through in the book. All tools and templates are available at my website, www.CorporateCrossovers.com/when-its-time. Look out for the download icon as you go through the book.

Why Corporate Crossovers®?

I know now, from my own experience and that of my clients, that the transition from being an employee to running your own business is massive. It is very rarely discussed. The change of role, income source, place of work, loss of colleagues and infrastructure are significant shifts. We have to learn how to run a business, sell, do marketing and a myriad of other tasks.

Internally, there are also significant changes. Identity, ego, views of our value and success become challenged as we crossover.

These shifts can be seismic and debilitating if not considered.

Redesigning a lifestyle, routine and daily rhythm we may have known for a decade or more is a monumental undertaking. As is reshaping our view of ourselves, what we value and how we have judged our success.

Examining these factors now, and being aware of the changes occurring will save you from coming unstuck later on. Knowledge of the shifts will fortify your commitment to crossing over.

In 2003, just after starting my business in Tokyo I was sitting in my home office. Staring out of the window over the rooftops, I had a fantasy. A sexy man in a red convertible would take me away from all of this. 'All of this' being running my own business. He would take me away and place me into a glamorous, well paid corporate job in a swanky office. I felt torn between working for myself and getting a job.

What moved me out of this inertia and completely stepping up and embracing my life as a Corporate Crossover was a thorough examination of my values, my success criteria and an honest appraisal of my past corporate life without the rose tinted spectacles.

It was this experience of painful seesawing between running my own business and getting a job that led me to create the Corporate Crossovers business and write this book.

Being armed with the knowledge that you will go through an internal transition process as you leave your corporate life to embark on life as a business owner, is essential to wholly commit to your chosen path. You must fully own what you are doing, let go of the past and embrace the future potential of your opportunity.

One thing I have learned over the years is that we evolve. Our values, what we are passionate about and the difference we make can all change over time. Eight years after I started my coaching business, I knew I still loved coaching and helping people exploit their potential but I started to question the value I was adding to my large corporate clients.

I realised that the culture of the organisation wasn't changing to support my client's changes they make through coaching, then over time their behaviour will slide, undoing all of their good work. Although my client would try to initiate positive changes after my coaching, these would only be temporary, as the culture of the organisation was resistant to change. I believe executive coaching in a toxic culture is like having an Alcoholics Anonymous meeting in a brewery; good intentions can only last so long in a bad environment.

My questions started me thinking about what I could focus on next, and at the same time I seemed to meet a number of women disenfranchised with their jobs, looking for something else. I also started working with more women business owners. I saw the importance of the coaching to these women. Their livelihood and that of their families depended on creating and sustaining successful and viable businesses. They would make the changes suggested in the coaching and sustain them because the benefits were evident and they were able to create an environment to support their change.

They were creating a new way of work that worked for them.

I have had the opportunity to work with thousands of Corporate Crossovers globally. The common element between them all is their desire to work in a way that respects their values and their intelligence, and to take control of their lives. You probably have a lot in common with these women.

I have also conducted much quantitative research in an effort to understand the Corporate Crossover, enjoyed over 50 in-depth interviews and spoken and worked with many women in their quest.

Wherever you are on your journey as a Corporate Crossover, this book will provide you with the fuel to create a business that allows you to live the life you love.

A reluctant Corporate Crossover

My story starts in rural New Zealand, where I grew up on a farm, seeing first-hand how capricious the industry could be. I saw my parents do well in the good times and then struggle when things got tough – bad weather, market oversupply, prices dropping, interest rates rising, squeezing cash flow and a seemingly limitless number of animals and crops to look after – no holidays allowed.

Dad thought my best job prospect was as a farmer's wife, and did his best to get me married off. But I refused – I knew there had to be something better out there. As luck would have it, I saw a job advertisement in the newspaper for something called 'marketing'. "Making commercials, designing packaging, selling products?" I thought. "This sounds more like me." I moved to the city and studied a marketing degree. When the opportunity arose to take a job in Sydney, I moved to Australia. Success there led me to a role in London, which gave me opportunities and income I could barely have imagined on the farm back in New Zealand.

My status and identity was firmly wrapped up in being a successful professional. I loved it, the travel, the opportunities and the people. Yes, I had had my son and wanted another child, one day, but staying at home with him was never an option I considered. My approach to childcare was: "Pay the right money and we will get the right solution." (Even as I write that I realise now, how much in the last ten years I have changed.)

Then, shock! My husband was offered the chance to do a three-year stint in Japan, which was sold to him to accelerate his career. I didn't want to move to Tokyo. I loved London and I loved my job. He was convinced it was the right decision. I wasn't impressed, why should I be the one to compromise my career?

Being conflict adverse and a solution finder, I avoided a showdown. With a spirit of open mindedness, I visited Tokyo and interviewed with a range of head-hunters. It seemed that I would get a job, though it would probably take a while.

So with that glimmer of hope, we moved to Japan.

Fast-forward four months. Sprawled on the floor, I am crying my heart out. I had no job, no hope of getting one, no income, and I didn't even know who I was any more. I was completely miserable. In that desperate moment, I decided to take my savings, leave my husband and son behind, and head back to London to the corporate world I loved.

But I didn't leave. I stayed in Tokyo and I stayed with my family. I accepted that I was not going to get a corporate job and that if I wanted to work then I would have to set up my own business and work for myself.

That is how I became a Corporate Crossover. Not really an inspiring start, I'll admit. Unwilling, unplanned and completely unexpected.

My toxic corporate environment

On the whole I had loved working in corporate. There were some great things about it:

- A regular pay check
- People to talk to every day
- Challenging and stimulating projects

But if I'm really honest, a few cracks had started appearing in my satisfied corporate veneer. Which, like fault lines, had been there all along but needed a tremor to open them up to be visible.

I was starting to question myself: Do I really care about the services our organisation was trying to create? What difference would they really make? I was also getting extremely frustrated by and caught up in the corporate politics. My integrity was challenged time and time again and I felt less comfortable about decisions taken by the executive team, of which I was part.

I felt I was wasting effort on initiating plans to save the business money – my ideas to scale down operations in speculative markets and increase profitability fell on deaf ears. I was very stressed, and regularly in tears after work.

Choosing the right career for myself

In my last year in London, I decided that I wanted something more than my job as a General Manager was giving me. Reviewing my past roles, I realised that I loved change. I loved moving countries, getting new jobs, launching new companies and projects. So, decision made! I would become a change management consultant.

This is what led me to decide to train as a coach. I needed to know how individuals dealt with change to enable them to manage it successfully. I never started the training expecting to have a coaching business. But when it finished and I realised that I wasn't going to get a job in Tokyo. I thought, "Damn it, if I can't get a job, I'll just start my own business and I 'll be a coach".

Two months on from sprawling miserably on the floor not knowing what to do with my life, I was running a business in an area that was completely new to me, in a foreign country with a limited network.

The second leg of the journey

After finally getting on with my life in Tokyo and creating a successful business, with a waiting list of coaching clients, my husband got the call to return to London. Just what I wanted – two years ago!

I left Tokyo with very fond memories and feeling grateful that we had gone there, for all I had discovered. As well as returning with a wonderful three-year-old son, we also bought back a beautiful baby daughter.

Back in London, I was plagued with indecision: should I stay self-employed or should I get real, and return to corporate life now I was back in my old stomping ground?

What drove this indecision?

- Loneliness – running your own company can be isolating
- The prospect of starting again – all the hard work to get up and running again in a new and more competitive market place
- The thought of not earning as much money as I used to in London

All the factors that make it hard to leave the corporate world in the first place were there, undermining my certainty and my confidence. As well as running my business, I started to interview for jobs.

It was 18 months until the indecision left me. I clearly remember the day I made the decision. I was upstairs in my office when Liberty, my two-year-old daughter called up, "Mummy, lunch is ready!" (My nanny had just cooked for us.) I had just added up my turnover and in eight months I had made more than the salary of my old job. Finally, the penny dropped, I had a great income doing what I loved, and able to easily have time with my children.

What a turning point that was. The energy consumed by not making a decision could now be channelled into something far more productive – making my business fly! I love what I do and get immense fulfilment from my work. My creativity is stimulated and I get to meet the most amazing people through my ventures. I am still on a journey as my business evolves and I learn and grow with it.

At times, it is hard work, frustrating, and all consuming. A decade on, I still have the occasional fantasy about the man in his red sports car whisking me off. And I now see that as a signal for when my business is going through radical change, not a sign to start interviewing for jobs again.

My business has been an enabler. Not only has it supported my family, but also it gave me the means and the freedom to fulfil a long held dream. For years, I dreamt of living in the South of France for six months and then traveling through Europe and the US in an RV with my family, all while running my business remotely. Last year, my dream came true!

1 Thinking of leaving your job?

What is it that ignites and stirs that desire for something different? Why do you consider leaving something you have known for many years? A place where you have spent so much of your time, an environment where you may have defended decisions you haven't truly supported, a place where you have met lifelong friends, even spouses, and where you have been paid, week in and week out.

What would make you consider such a radical change? One that may leave you questioning your confidence, wondering who you are, close to the verge of bankruptcy and losing it all. Giving up weekends, forgoing your down-time, your mind always churning as your business consumes you twenty-four hours a day, seven days a week.

What is it that stirs the winds of change? And makes you become a Corporate Crossover, leaving your life as an employee to become an entrepreneur? The ignition for that fire, and the catalysts for change, are different for everyone. Every situation is very personal, based on our individual values and circumstances.

> But there is one thing we all have in common: there comes a point in our lives where we just can't take it anymore.

The desire to leave and pursue our own business may have been bubbling in the back of our minds for a while. Then a switch flips, or a series of events cascade, and the decision suddenly becomes obvious.

1

You realise:

- There must be more to my life than this.
- I want to be in control of my destiny.
- I value my flexibility and autonomy over any job, salary or title.
- My core values are not represented at the place where I spend most of my time.
- I could have a better life and I can create it for myself.

As your heart and mind become open to the possibility of leaving – you start to consider what a new way of work could be like. Events (such as redundancy, children, a move, a new boss, a restructure or an illness) may conspire to push you further away from your workplace. Events like these can change your perspective on what matters in your life. They can give you that push you need to take the plunge, and start the journey of being a Corporate Crossover.

The surprising results of my research

Why do women leave their jobs to start their own businesses? Every woman has a different story, but when I conducted my own research, the results surprised me – there are definitely some common themes.

Recently I conducted a large quantitative survey, polling 300 women from the UK and the US who had left their jobs to create their own businesses. In the online survey, they answered questions about why they left their jobs. They also told me what they loved, and found challenging about running their businesses. It was an impressive group of entrepreneurs; the media picked up on the research results and I was featured on the BBC and in HR magazines worldwide.

The three main reasons that women left their jobs:

1. To escape a toxic workplace culture
2. To be in control of their own destinies

3. To have the freedom to choose how to spend their time.

Contrary to what you might imagine, few women left their jobs because they had a burning desire to start their own company or launch a new product.

> They saw their businesses as a means to an end – a way to generate income, do something meaningful and leave a stressful corporate environment.

So if you would like to be your own boss, control your own destiny and escape your job, don't assume that you need to wait for a lightning bolt of inspiration to strike.

Another surprising result of my research was that only one per cent of respondents cited the glass ceiling as a reason for their departure. For most it was the toxic culture that ultimately drove them to leave. It's as if each of these women woke up one day and realised, 'I am worth more than this'. They see they have other options that will be more fulfilling and will allow them to live the way they want to. Whether through frustration or life events, the scales fall from their eyes and they decide to cross over.

The toxic workplace

The women in my study usually had both a 'push' and a 'pull' desire – the 'push' to escape the toxic culture of their current workplace and the 'pull' of independence and freedom.

What is the toxic culture that suffocates so many women in the workplace, that causes them to take the leap and crossover? The culture of toxicity is made up of many elements:

- Corporate politics
- Decisions overturned

- Bureaucracy
- Back-stabbing
- Opaque decision-making
- Paying lip service to the company values
- Incompetent leadership
- Hampered innovation

- Extreme pressure
- Long hours
- Presenteeism
- Unrealistic demands
- Deadlines and budgets
- No appreciation of staff and effort... The list goes on.

A poisonous mix that you can endure for a surprisingly long time, and then you know it's time to get out and save yourself. For me, it was the sheer frustration of turning up to another pointless meeting where decisions are made and then overturned for no seemingly good reason.

In one of my last corporate roles, as General Manager, I was ultimately responsible for appointing our branding agency. A thorough briefing and selection process had been conducted and a decision had been made with all members of the executive team buying in and giving it their support, including the company president. Or so I thought.

In the following week, before the kick-off meeting with the selected agency (a leader in global branding) the president walked into my office and directed me to brief and use another agency that hadn't even made the shortlist. Two weeks before Christmas.

No reason supplied; just that 'Bob' thinks it's a good idea. Bob, who had sat in the meeting the week before agreeing overtly with the decision. Bob, who had more power over our boss than anyone, even the CEO. Scrambling into action (I knew I would be wasting my breath trying to get my boss to change his mind), I did what I was told and briefed the new agency. I wasn't prepared to risk the project on Bob's opinion so I kept the original agency informed and didn't cut the ties. I was totally transparent with them. Bob's agency didn't deliver on the

Chapter 1: Thinking of leaving your job?

pitch as well as the agency I had selected so we went back with my original recommendation. Two weeks of high stress, emotion and time wasted because of Bob.

Dee held various senior marketing roles in the movie industry including at Momentum Pictures in London, Paramount Pictures in Los Angeles and Focus Features, a division of Universal Pictures, in New York': "I loved what I did, [but] the politics in some places can be overwhelming and soul-destroying. 'It can turn you into someone you don't want to be'. Because if you're smart and you understand corporate culture you know how to play the game. To some people it's just routine that's what they do, they say the right things, they 'align themselves with' the right people, and are very smooth. But for others, there's a point at which you just hit a wall and you think there must be more than this. I just want to do the work."

The kudos of spending time with actors and filmmakers and the thrill of working on movies she loved, was no longer enough to outweigh the fact that her friendships were disintegrating as she gave up birthdays and holidays for work. She had very little time to spend with her friends as she surrendered all her time and energy to her employers. Daily life moved at a frantic pace as she travelled extensively – the demands of corporate culture pushed her away from her job while the dream of flexibility pulled her in to starting her own business.

Dee left the corporate world and started Right Angle – and it wasn't an easy journey. Cash flow was a major obstacle when she began, and at one point, necessity meant she applied for a full-time job. She didn't get it, which she now sees as a blessing; "failure is part of the journey". Her businesses are now thriving, and Dee loves the fact that her achievements are all her own; "I'm fearless now."

Many of you will have a Bob in your own working life. And whether it is an experience like that, or an ongoing series of smaller events, they affect us. They eat away at our self-esteem, our belief in what's right and ultimately can leave us questioning our ability.

I have heard similar stories from the many women I have spoken to during my research. One of my favourites is from Dee Poku, co-founder and CEO of Women: Inspiration and Enterprise (WIE) and Right Angle, a marketing consultancy.

Controlling your own destiny

For Dee, it was a nearly-cancelled holiday to Cuba that was the wake-up call she needed. The events that life thrust upon you can give you cause to reflect and question your current circumstances. It may be an illness, a sudden death, a sick child, a marriage breakdown or an unexpected event that will spark an inspection of your current circumstances.

> You become less tolerant and start feeling that your life is worth more than this.

You become frustrated that you aren't living your dream. You wonder if this is really worth it. You start to reflect where you are at, and begin an honest assessment.

Suddenly, the endless meetings and arguments over decisions seem petty and irrelevant to the larger meaning of our lives. Having children can change our perspective on office politics. It can be this realisation that wakes women up to embark on a new path.

Wanting to leave your mark on the world and creating a business representing your values can also be a key driver for many women. Some feel that in a corporate environment their values are not represented and their creativity and impact are stifled. Stunted. Repressed. They feel they are living a half-life. Tolerating the culture of the organisation when they are at conflict with its norms and behaviours. They feel frustrated as their creativity and passion is thwarted as the corporate machine rolls on.

"I wanted more freedom and felt that I could make a bigger impact in the world on my own rather than in the confines of the corporate office," commented one woman in the study. Another respondent echoed that sense of being unable to stretch her wings: "I had major frustration about not being able to implement my ideas. I was not doing what I am passionate about. I was using my skills to make someone else money. I don't like being told what to do. I wanted more freedom to decide how I use my time."

> Galia Orme wanted more meaning in her work. She had a long and successful career in sales and marketing. Her last job was in business development for an online marketing consultancy.
>
> "I felt that the company I was working for wasn't valuing the work I was doing or my contributions to their business. I was bringing in more money than anyone else in the business, earning the least and not being promoted. After I hit 40, I thought, 'it's time for me'. I wanted to do something for myself, something that I can be proud of, that I've achieved in terms of my work career. I left just after my fortieth birthday. I simply resigned, without knowing exactly what I was going to do."
>
> Galia didn't know what her business would be, but she knew she wanted to set up something that was ethical and meaningful. She ultimately founded CHOC Chick, a premium raw chocolate company that allowed her to take her marketing skills and apply them to something she was passionate about and had a real impact on the lives of her suppliers. Her products are now stocked in many of the premium retail outlets throughout the UK and Europe.

Why do we need our life to be turned upside down before we make steps to improve it? Why do we need an external catalyst to mobilise us to give it a go? It's not complacency.

It's balancing the perceived risk of starting up our business against putting up and tolerating the situation we have now.

We are always subconsciously balancing this equation in our minds. "Should I stay, or should I go now?" If we don't love the answer we get back, we start to consider leaving.

A recent Corporate Crossover describes it like this: "I spent 20 years of my life in a corporate environment. It never allowed me to follow my purpose. Leaving took me through the change cycle of the normal fears: Will I earn enough, will I find work, am I good enough or just fooling myself? Once I was out of the corporate environment, I felt that the window to the world opened up for me and I could finally create the life I wanted. I also realised that we hold ourselves back because of our fears or waiting for the 'one day when' scenario to play, which stops us from living our dream and loving life."

Freedom and flexibility

We hear the niggling and gentle prodding that not all is right with our world but sometimes it is easier to ignore this than to delve deeper. Ignoring means we can continue on, risk free. This works well until an external event causes us to stop, reflect and ponder. We give ourselves the permission to reflect, assess and possibly set a new path.

It makes us realise that our comfort zone is uncomfortable and we don't want to tolerate it any longer. Some of us can just cease to

Chapter 1: Thinking of leaving your job?

function. After working hard for many years, our bodies can just say, "ENOUGH!".

> Susan Moore was Senior Executive Assistant to a CEO of a major bank, before a medical problem made her re-evaluate her life:
>
> "I had two small children and I spent a lot of time away from home, so I was out of the door at six in the morning and back home at eight at night. I had two under-twos and they were just at nursery school. Then I discovered I had a brain tumour. I was very lucky, it was benign and it was operable. I started to think I don't want to work like this anymore, because I'm never at home. It was just all work and no fun, really. The tumour pulled me up and made me think about my life".
>
> The brain tumour made Susan think hard about her priorities – did she want to be away from her young children so much? She left her job and founded Moore Virtual Assistance, a premium virtual assistance company, that has become a leader in its niche. Susan is still extremely busy, but she is able to set her own terms and spend time with her children.

Julie Anixter, Co-Founder and Executive Editor at Innovation Excellence sums this up; "You're leaving because you have a dream about a better life, a better way to live and that dream is worth taking very seriously."

THE JOURNEY TO BECOME
A CORPORATE CROSSOVER

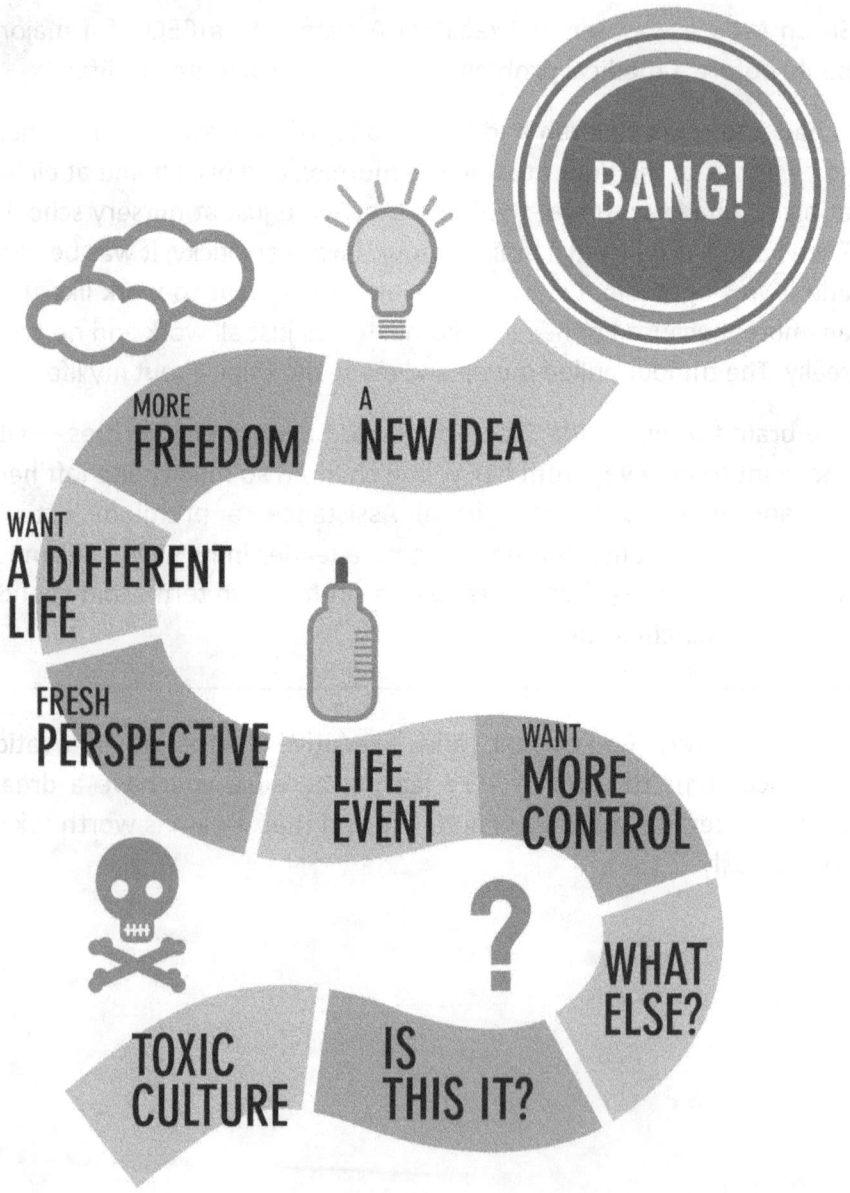

BANG!

A NEW IDEA

MORE FREEDOM

WANT A DIFFERENT LIFE

FRESH PERSPECTIVE

LIFE EVENT

WANT MORE CONTROL

?

WHAT ELSE?

TOXIC CULTURE

IS THIS IT?

Chapter 1: Thinking of leaving your job?

As you travel through the path towards becoming a Corporate Crossover, the big question emerges: "Should I stay, or should I go?" The question begins as a whisper and then over time, the volume increases and becomes more persistent, demanding an answer.

In your head, an equation starts to formulate which eventually gives you the answer. The equation gets calculated many times over the journey. One day you do the equation and realise that there is no longer any value in staying. The question is answered and you decide to leave.

THE SHOULD I STAY OR SHOULD I GO NOW EQUATION

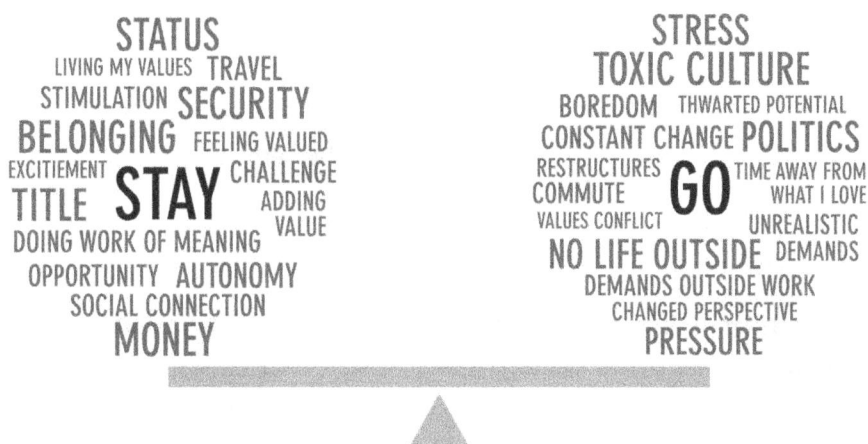

STATUS
LIVING MY VALUES TRAVEL
STIMULATION SECURITY
BELONGING FEELING VALUED
EXCITIEMENT STAY CHALLENGE
TITLE ADDING
DOING WORK OF MEANING VALUE
OPPORTUNITY AUTONOMY
SOCIAL CONNECTION
MONEY

STRESS
TOXIC CULTURE
BOREDOM THWARTED POTENTIAL
CONSTANT CHANGE POLITICS
RESTRUCTURES GO TIME AWAY FROM
COMMUTE WHAT I LOVE
VALUES CONFLICT UNREALISTIC
NO LIFE OUTSIDE DEMANDS
DEMANDS OUTSIDE WORK
CHANGED PERSPECTIVE
PRESSURE

Depending on the woman and her situation, the weighing up can happen very quickly or it may take years. There can be a variety of influences that finally tip the scales in favour of leaving.

"I spent three years applying for other positions and I hit that point, a level of frustration, so that I really had to move from where I was," one respondent told me. "I'm currently working on establishing new business options and activities."

Is it time to go?

What is it that finally makes us leave? To make the decision to go, to take the redundancy package and not look for a new job, or never to return after an absence?

What crystallises our thinking to make such a decision that will affect our lives, our livelihoods and reshape our view of who we are and what's important to us?

Based on my research it is more likely to be a slow burn of continual questioning (What else could I do?) and then a realisation that the time is now, or it will never happen.

An internal reckoning that:

- there is more to life than this
- I am worth more than this
- what I have been thinking of doing is preferable to staying

The perceived benefits of leaving definitely outweigh staying. So they leave.

Redundancy can also bring that slow burn to a head. If you have been frustrated for a while, retrenchment can come as a welcome relief. As one respondent comments; "Although I loved the job I did, I took voluntary redundancy. I was fed up with the politics and the constant reinventing of the wheel within the company."

> For some, the smouldering dissatisfaction can lead to a spark, igniting the conversation that leads to the quitting their job.

It's as if another political fight, overseas flight or insensitive comment pushes them over the edge, turns into a bolt of energy and they make the decision to leave!

Chapter 1: Thinking of leaving your job?

It is a catalytic moment. Sometimes a catalytic moment can also be triggered by an external event.

> One Corporate Crossover remembers: "I had been thinking to do something else for a while. The crunch moment came for me the Monday after the Bali bombings in 2002. Working in PR we had planned to launch a press release that day about the launch of a new chocolate variety in a well-known chocolate range. I knew that the timing was not appropriate as the world's media was all focused on the bombings and that getting coverage of a new chocolate variant would be slim. I rang my client early that morning and shared with her my recommendation to delay the launch. She disagreed. She couldn't understand my point of view. That day I realised I wanted to quit PR and do something more meaningful to me."

Frustration, anger, stress, disappointment and feeling constrained by the norms of corporate life. Emotions build up and the most obvious choice is to leave.

To take control of your destiny, to create a legacy and directly feel the impact you can make.

Ultimately you find yourself spending more time at work wishing you weren't there than actually working. Your attention is piqued by the stories of other women who have crossed over and succeeded, and you wonder more and more what it would be like to do the same.

> For Laura Bergerson it was a slow burn and then a realisation that she could make a change. Her insight came when she realised that others would pay her for the same work.

"I worked in the channels organization for a high tech company for about six years and I was becoming unhappy in my job. It didn't matter how much pay they gave me, how much freedom I had or whatever they offered me. I began to realise that the culture wasn't working for me anymore. One day I thought, 'If my employer pays me money to do this, probably other people will pay me money to do this too'."

Laura was right. She became the founder and CEO of Channel Impact and Talent Impact; two companies which are leaders in sales promotion for technology companies.

Your push and your pull

Only you can understand the strength of the push – those aspects of your current job that make you want to leave – and the strength of the pull – your desire to run your own business. But by carefully analysing both forces, you can work out whether it's truly time for you to cross over from the corporate world into the world of an entrepreneur.

2 What you'll need to succeed

After 11 years of having my own business, and working with thousands of Corporate Crossovers, I know running your own business is an intense personal development experience. This is not what we expect when we crossover from our jobs into entrepreneurship.

Running your own business involves a steep and continuous learning curve.

Once you've started your own company, there will likely be times when difficult situations cause you to rethink your decision. Chasing late payments, missed deadlines due to supplier problems, losing customers – these are the kind of events which cause you to take stock, learn and ensure you find ways to prevent a recurrence.

It's not only external happenings that encourage you to grow and learn new skills and approaches, but your self-confidence is challenged. You now have to sell yourself as well as your product. You need to be able to walk into a room of strangers at networking events and muster the courage to do what needs to be done to grow your business. Large and small set-backs can rob you of that confidence.

Even if you used to do all of this when you were working in your previous job, somehow, doing it under your own business banner can be intimidating. You can feel even more judged and uncertain of your strengths. Your inner voice gets louder, dissuading you from action and causing you to procrastinate and become stuck.

Running your own business is a very rewarding and exhilarating experience. But in reality it's much harder than anyone tells you.

What is it like to run your own business? Is it really the entrepreneurial dream? Do customers come flocking to you as soon as you open your doors? Do you have the time to create the life of your dreams?

Sadly, the answer is no. I've spoken with many Corporate Crossovers* and they have consistently told me the same story: "I didn't realise just how hard it would be to start my own business and then to make it viable". Having your own business and making it a success will call on your deepest resources of resilience, commitment to the idea, your energy and tenacity.

So if you have been feeling the winds of change stir, could you do it? Could you leave your job and create your own business? Have you got what it takes? What are those qualities that make a Corporate Crossover successful?

The good news is that you have all the qualities you need to succeed.

What has made you successful in your career to date will ultimately make you successful as you embark on your new journey.

Running your own business will tease dormant qualities out of you. Building your new venture, you will learn more about yourself and how you work than at any other time of your life. As you embark on your journey of crossing over, and even years into it, you will still be questioning yourself, the volume of brain chat and self-criticism will increase but, ultimately, you will be surprised by your determination, tenacity and resilience.

Seven essential qualities

The Corporate Crossovers I spoke with recognised that they had some potent personal attributes. By the time I had interviewed over 300 women, I found that there were seven characteristics that set Corporate Crossovers apart:

THE 7 ESSENTIAL QUALITIES OF A SUCCESSFUL CORPORATE CROSSOVER

Everyone has these skills to some extent, and you will be stronger in some of these areas than others. But if you are prepared to exploit your strengths and develop your weaknesses, there's no reason you can't become a very successful Corporate Crossover.

Passion

You need a total and utter belief that what you are doing is worth it.

A feeling of being so in love with your idea and the value it will bring to others that you can feel it.

A strong reason why. Why you are doing this, why it exists and why it's worth it. Even when you doubt yourself, you won't want to go back.

Donna Sturgess is the founder and CEO of Buyology, an innovative marketing consultancy. She left a very senior role at GlaxoSmithKline after a successful 30-year career there. Donna explains that she deliberately chose to leave her corporate role, and to choose a business she was truly passionate about.

"If your passion does not show up in your start-up, it is bloody hard work. If you're not passionate with what you're doing, it isn't easy on any given day. And when it's hard you will throw your arms up and go.... 'What am I doing? This is a hard way to make a living'."

You will be working on this business, like it or not, twenty-four hours a day, seven days a week. Whether or not you are physically sitting down and working, your thoughts will be occupied with your business. It becomes all-consuming, so you'd better love what you do! High levels of passion for what you are creating will fuel you. Equally important is to be passionate about running your own business – passionate about being in charge, making the decisions and operating a business.

Having your own business is not a job. You will put more of your heart and soul into it than you thought possible. Like it or not, you have to approach it as a new way of life. If you don't give it 100%, you will only earn an income, never build a business. Building a business requires you to constantly stretch and challenge yourself.

Having complete and utter passion for your business will fuel you as you battle with your internal fears and stretch out of your comfort

Chapter 2: What you'll need to succeed

zone. Running your own business will require you to do new tasks and activities, some that will require a large dose of confidence. If you have the passion, this is much easier.

How does it feel when you are around someone who has a high level of energy and is passionate about what they are discussing? It feels great. It's infectious. You want some of what they have. This is the passion I'm talking about, the feeling you have when you spend time on what you really care about, the thing that makes your heart sing.

> You not only have to be passionate about what you do, you also have to be passionate about building a successful and profitable business.

This passion for success leads onto the other six vital qualities.

Emma Arkell was a very successful lawyer in a top London law firm, earning a high income. She traded that to start Emma Arkell Aromatherapy, and she believes that passion has been one of the biggest factors in her success: "Don't just try and do something for the sake of doing something. If you're not passionate about it you won't succeed. You've got to have that energy and that interest and you've got to put so much of yourself into it, you have to love it."

Determination

You must have the determination to make your business a success, to persevere when it seems that luck is against you, and to do whatever it takes to build the business. Many people may begin businesses but not all succeed; those who do are those who keep persevering. You cannot give up at the first, third or even the tenth rejection; you must carry on until you get what you want. You know that a 'yes' is key to the success of your business and realisation of your passion, so you don't give up until you get it.

Having utter conviction that your business deserves to be a success will drive your determination. You will have difficult times, and doubt yourself, but if you start with this conviction it will get you through.

Galia Orme of CHOC Chick remembers a time when her determination was tested to the limit. She had created a premium raw chocolate making kit, and she needed to have her product stocked at the right retailers to match the brand and the pricing. She had her sights set on nationwide UK premium retailers in particular.

"Getting into the high-end national retail chain was the big challenge for me, it took me a year overall. I called the buyer for three months, phoning him nearly every day, leaving him messages and sometimes just calling and hanging up, and then one day he finally picked up the phone and agreed to meet with me."

After three months, when he finally answered, he said to me, "I don't think anyone's ever been this persistent, did you realise I could see your number every time you called?" That strategy worked, and it kept on working. CHOC Chick products are now stocked in Harvey Nichols, Whole Foods Market, John Lewis Food Halls, Magasin du Nord Denmark and Chelsea Market Baskets in New York among others.

Galia's determination might seem extreme, but she's actually typical of a Corporate Crossover woman. These women are unflagging in their determination and persistence, whether they're aiming to get listed in a retailer, to land that big-name client or to get the funding they require to start.

Determination and persistence for these Corporate Crossovers develops to a level beyond what they had in their jobs. Getting what you want for your business becomes all encompassing. Fueled by the belief that you will ultimately succeed, your commitment is unwavering and it keeps you going until you achieve your objective.

> When it is your own business and you need to create a sustainable income and business entity, you will push yourself further than when you were employed.

Being even moderately successful in your career will mean you already have some determination. Taking this to the next level to call a national retail buyer every day for three months, or to conduct 119 meetings before your first sale, requires the kind of determination which will set your business apart from the thousands which fail every year.

Julie Meyer MBE, Chairman and Chief Executive – Ariadne Capital; Managing Partner – Ariadne Fund; and Founder – Entrepreneur Country talks about her experience: "It was July 2006 and I was at a cocktail party in Monaco. It was about nine pm when I got a text from Alastair Lukies, the founder of Monitise, now worth £2 billion, and it said, '119 meetings, 79 nights away from my wife, but today Monitise has a meeting.' That's not normal. That's obsession."

Optimism

You don't need to be Pollyanna; every Corporate Crossover I spoke to experienced setbacks – rejection, slower than forecast sales, unexpected disasters. They were down, but not out. When things didn't go well, they used their optimism to drive them to find an alternative strategy for success. Optimistic Corporate Crossovers reflect on their successes instead of their failures. They also look for the benefits and opportunities in every situation, thinking of their business goal and how the situation can enhance it. They will see opportunities where others see only problems.

Taking the difficulties and mistakes and learning from them is an essential quality of a successful Corporate Crossover. Having a victim mentality will not support you or the growth of your business. Completely owning that you make your business happen and that it will be a success is an enabling mindset. A sense of optimism will enable you to revisit your passion and then think 'What if there was another way?' and 'How can we get past this?'"

> Remember that while you can't control what happens to you, you can control how you react to it.

Optimism helps you to seek the possibilities in life. It gives you a mindset of growth and forward thinking. Rather than dwelling on past mistakes and maybes, you can think about 'What could happen...?' and 'How can I...?' You can be constantly reviewing and learning and looking for better ways to do things.

Maria Johnson, founder of Eddie Catz, a chain of indoor play centres for young children, managed to channel her optimism into success when most people would have wilted. During a hot, sunny summer in London, her customer numbers dwindled; children preferred to play outdoors rather than come inside. "We had one summer that was so hard, we thought 'Oh my goodness what are we going to do?' We bought a popcorn and a candy floss machine and we set up in the park nearby. We really became very proactive. That really difficult year served its purpose," and Maria has been using some of these creative marketing techniques ever since, with great results.

Optimism will also fuel your activity. If you believe that you control your environment and make things happen when you are out there, you will always create opportunities and momentum. You will make that difference in the world that so many of our Corporate Crossovers hope to make when they leave their jobs. Holding onto that attitude means you will attract more opportunities and chances to make your business grow and succeed.

Customer love

Business is all about people. Critical to any successful business is an attitude of customer love. This means not only forming great relationships with prospects, but also forging stronger relationships as they become customers. Many of the women I spoke to emphasised the importance of developing deep and strong relationships with all customers. They enjoyed long-term client relationships and these also resulted in new customer referrals.

> They took pride in their work and went the extra mile to ensure that every customer was delighted so they didn't start to consider competitors.

They believe that building a strong relationship with customers is critical.

Zoe Sinclair of Employees Matter, an educational company for employees, formerly a producer at the BBC, discusses her version of customer love: "Whether you are a business owner dealing with the public or dealing one on one with clients, my mantra has been 'under promise and over deliver.' I really followed that because I think that clients and the public, whoever buys your services, whoever you work for, will always remember that you've over delivered on something."

This is a key switch from life in the corporate environment. Running your own business means you are the front line of customer service.

Your income comes from your customers. This may sound obvious, but it can be overlooked after an extended period in corporate, where customer experiences are managed by a customer service department, or fed via a market research report or filtered through the sales department.

But this is part of the joy (and some of the stress) of having your own company. Direct contact with customers and choosing who you work with is a common source of enjoyment among the women I surveyed. They loved being in control of who they interacted with and being directly involved with them.

> Delivering great service to the customer and consistently exceeding their expectations not only makes great business sense but, importantly, feeds the flame of your professional passion.

Knowing your clients will feed your desire to build strong relationships with your customers, and this becomes a natural part of your business strategy, not something enforced by adhering to metrics or service level agreements. Messages of customer delight can encourage and motivate you, especially at those times when your enthusiasm wanes.

Karen Silk worked in sales for a major manufacturer of laboratory equipment, before making the leap to become the managing director of Capital International Staffing, a large recruitment firm. She is passionate about engaging with her clients: "We focus very strongly on customer service, we constantly look at new ideas and new ways to do things. We have lots of debates and discussions about how we can change or improve our service. Encourage your staff to be part of and committed to the whole concept of delivering well to the customer." This approach has been hugely successful for Karen, who was recently invited to join the Representative Committee of APSCO (The Association of Professional Staffing Companies).

Flexibility

Staying close to your customers also means that you are that much more informed about their needs and how the market may be shifting. In many cases the business you start may be different to one that you are running a few years later. The need to be nimble (and, therefore, observant) is an essential quality.

"I'd say keep open to the organic nature of your business because your market will tell you where to go. The market is organic, your customers are real people and they change and evolve. I think in order for a business to do well, you have to be really open to change and not be afraid of it," advises Laura Bergerson, founder of Channel Impact, a channel consultancy in Silicon Valley; and Talent Impact, a direct hire staffing firm.

Closer relationships to the customer also means a faster and more accurate feedback loop for the business. Adjustments can be made quickly to better service customers, new product development cycle times are reduced as you act directly on feedback and the resultant opportunity. It also allows you close and direct market intelligence, giving you an understanding of your competitors' activities, market trends, dynamics and shifts, allowing you to adapt your business strategy accordingly.

Flexibility and the ability to alter the business to meet the needs of the market is key.

This is not about running after the latest shiny new thing because everyone else is doing it; but really knowing your market, understanding your customers' needs and creating products and services to meet them. As your business evolves, you will learn much more about your area and your customer niche. Take this learning and apply it to your business to add real value.

A strong work ethic

When you are setting up your business, you are creating something out of nothing. You are establishing a brand in a competitive market place, creating a presence, building a sales pipeline; getting prospects to know, like and trust you and your offering.

Starting up your own business can feel like you are working harder than ever before. As you become established, you may be working the longest hours of your life, and earning far less money than in your previous job. This stage of building the business is like getting a jumbo jet off the ground. You need far more fuel and energy to get that behemoth off the ground than when you are cruising comfortably at 35,000 feet.

Former BBC producer Zoe Sinclair works hard as the founder and director of Employees Matter: "I work every hour that I can possibly manage when I'm not with the children. I live and breathe my own company now, I wake up in the morning thinking about it, I go to bed at night thinking about it, it's mine. You know it's a real shift in your mind, it's the total responsibility."

But this hard work has paid off handsomely for Zoe. While two-thirds of the women surveyed were yet to get back to their corporate income levels, Zoe is one of the third who earns more than in her previous roles. Her company has presented seminars to over 10,000 people, and Zoe was awarded the Red Hot Women in Business award in 2010.

For many Corporate Crossovers, the level of stress, the level of perseverance, the level of dedication, is much more difficult, than what they encountered when they had a job. Whilst they may have started their business with the objective of an even work-life balance, often the scales are tipped heavily on the work side for several years.

Yet their determination, passion and utter belief fuels them through this. Their intense love of what they do keeps them working at these extreme levels. They are prepared to earn less and work harder and longer than their staff.

> They put the needs of the business ahead of their own.

Courage

Opportunities are everywhere but you have to be courageous to grab them. Founding and running your own business will push and pull at every part of your comfort zone. You will have to put yourself out there in ways you haven't imagined. There is no company or brand to lean on anymore and no sales department to bring in the business. It is now completely up to you.

Tenacity is closely linked to courage. Making the cold call to a key prospect will require you to be tenacious. And then following up not once, but maybe five or ten times, until you reach them and get an answer.

Successful Corporate Crossovers have let go of many things. They have let go of the fear of rejection, the fear of being seen as too direct, the fear of selling and asking for the order. Once these fears have gone, they become tenacious, motivated and gain momentum.

> Having courage will allow you find more opportunities and ultimately result in more business.

It is that sense that if I have nothing now and try, and fail, then nothing has been lost, and you know you have tried. But if you give it a go and it succeeds, then you not only get what you wanted but your confidence increases. Remember that old adage: "If you don't ask, you don't get".

Emma Arkell left the high-earning world of divorce law to be her own boss at Emma Arkell Aromatherapy: "I think being self-employed, you've got to be robust, you've got to have a punchy nature, and have a feisty, strong personality to deal with the highs and the lows."

3 Are YOU cut out for it?

Before you leap to cross over, take some time to reflect on how you compare with the seven qualities outlined. When considering a new future, it is essential to deeply ponder why you are doing it. Is the reason big enough to deeply fuel your passion, tenacity and to motivate you to be brave?

Once you have had a chance to reflect on this, then consider how you compare against the seven essential qualities. Ask yourself, where are you now and where do you need to grow?

Remember, owning your own business is like an intense, never-ending personal development programme.

Exercise: How do you compare with the Seven Essential Qualities?

We now know what the Seven Essential Qualities are for a successful Corporate Crossover. How do you compare against the Seven Essential Qualities? Take some time for an honest reflection of where you are at.

You can download the worksheet to accompany this exercise at www.corporatecrossovers.com/when-its-time

Quality 1: Passion

- How much do you exhibit this quality?
- Score x/10
- Example of using it
- What score would you like to grow to?
- What could you do differently to increase your score?

Quality 2: Determination

- How much do you exhibit this quality?
- Score x/10
- Example of using it
- What score would you like to grow to?
- What could you do differently to increase your score?

Quality 3: Optimism

- How much do you exhibit this quality?
- Score x/10
- Example of using it
- What score would you like to grow to?
- What could you do differently to increase your score?

Quality 4: Customer love

- How much do you exhibit this quality?
- Score x/10
- Example of using it
- What score would you like to grow to?
- What could you do differently to increase your score?

Quality 5: Flexibility

- How much do you exhibit this quality?
- Score x/10
- Example of using it
- What score would you like to grow to?
- What could you do differently to increase your score?

Quality 6: Strong work ethic

- How much do you exhibit this quality?
- Score x/10
- Example of using it
- What score would you like to grow to?
- What could you do differently to increase your score?

Quality 7: Courage

- How much do you exhibit this quality?
- Score x/10
- Example of using it
- What score would you like to grow to?
- What could you do differently to increase your score?

Does this make you feel more confident, or are there areas that need a little development before you cross over?

Assessing where you are now and how you have already demonstrated aspects of each quality will provide you with a base from which to grow. I know that awareness is the first step to change. Being aware of how we operate now, and creating an objective of how we want to shift our behaviour, will help us get there.

Questions to consider...

1. What are the key points you have learned about yourself after assessing yourself against The Seven Essential Qualities?

2. What is your strongest quality?

3. Where do you need to develop?

4. What can you start to do today?

What makes you tick?

Running your own business will give you cause to examine those deeper recesses of your mind. As you go through the transition from employee to business owner, you will be stretching your comfort zone and pushing past any previous self-imposed limits. The truth is, this never stops.

> To grow your business, you will grow yourself.

Have you ever considered what makes you tick? What are those driving forces that make you who you are? Self-awareness can help us understand ourselves more and realise why we act as we do.

From my experience, prior events shape our thinking and create a framework from which we instinctively operate. Once we understand what this framework is, we get clarity on how we operate and a deeper understanding of why we do what we do.

Discover what makes you tick by completing this exercise. You will get the opportunity to reflect on significant events in your life and understand what has shaped your current view of the world.

Chapter 3: Are YOU cut out for it?

Exercise: What Makes Me Tick?

Take 30 minutes out and go somewhere you won't be interrupted; a quiet place where you can contemplate in peace. Take a notebook and pen.

You can download the worksheet to accompany this exercise at www.corporatecrossovers.com/when-its-time

Step 1: Key Events

Look back over your life to date and consider what have been seven key events that you think have shaped your thinking. They could be happy moments – moments of extreme pride or joy. They may also be sad moments – events when you were hurt deeply or disappointed.

The events can be from when you were a child, something at school or tertiary education. Maybe it was something that happened to you in your personal life as an adult, or even at work. What are those events that impacted you, positively or negatively, and shaped your view of the world and of yourself? What are those events that have shifted your thinking?

Think about those seven events over the course of your life that have shaped how you see the world. As you think about each event, write down in detail what happened, and how it made you feel.

Then ask yourself: "Why is this significant? How did this shape or change me?" And look deeply, as the first answer will be the easy one. Look much deeper to really see how it has shaped you and your thinking. Consider the event and probe deeply into why it has impacted you, and how it has formed any of the beliefs that you hold today.

Ask yourself these questions:

1. Why was the event significant?
2. How did it shape or change me?
3. How did it impact my thinking or view of the world then?
4. 4. What residual impact does that event have on me now?

Step 2: Review your events

Read through your list, ponder and observe what thoughts and feelings come up for you. Do you need to add anything else?

Step 3: Pull out the key themes

Now you have your seven events and how they have impacted you and your thinking, review the list again and see if you notice any themes. What recurring patterns are there? What do you think are the drivers from this list that have shaped who you are today?

As we embark on change, knowledge of this framework can help us make sense of the internal barriers we encounter or, conversely, why some things are so easy for us.

To help you with your understanding of what makes you tick, here are my experiences.

Step 1 and 2: My key events and their impact:

1. My mother being highly distressed about money when I was three, after my father's death; and again at 20, when she was upset about her farming business losing money. Of course as a three-year-old I would have been sad about my Mum crying. But the deeper impression that left on me, was how important financial security is. That belief has shaped my life, as for a very long time, I was terrified I would be a bag lady and end up on

the streets when I was old. I have spent a lot of time and energy working on this self-belief, but every now and again it does loom. I am now conscious of my deep need for financial security, of how it drives me and what decisions I make.

2. Discovering, as a teenager, my friends were having a party and I hadn't been invited. I realised that I never really fitted into a group of friends at my small town school. I felt terribly hurt that I had been left out, and it firmed my resolve that I would leave that town as soon as possible. I realise, in hindsight, my needing to leave was to prove to them that I was worth liking.

3. Receiving a promotion at Colgate Palmolive and moving from New Zealand to Australia when I was 22. This was multi-faceted in its meaning for me. I was immensely proud of my promotion, particularly as I was told that it would not be possible by my then marketing director. So I had 'won' in my mind. Coupled with this was the knowledge that I would be leaving New Zealand and my life living overseas was finally starting. I was primed for excitement and adventure.

4. At 25, walking onto the 747 jet in Sydney going to Hong Kong with a one-way ticket, leaving my long-term boyfriend and my safe job and not knowing what I would be doing or where I would travel. In my heart, adventure beckoned. I also knew that I had enough savings to last 12 months and that my CV was strong enough to get a job. I relished the freedom and my autonomy. The significance of this was that I did what I wanted to do, not what I 'should' have done. The safe thing to do would have been to stay in my 'good' job and get married.

5. A colleague trying to take the credit for a product launch I had developed and implemented in record time to enter the market against a competitive threat. This made me realise the importance of claiming your ideas as your own and recognising the importance of subtle self-promotion. This helped me learn

how to talk about myself in a positive way to the people that mattered. I also had deep anger at letting it happen in the first place and being walked over by this colleague.

6. Accepting that my husband may never work again, and I will continue to be the sole breadwinner for our family. This realisation steeled my determination to make my business a success and also to keep having many networks around the world for support, advice and ideas. It also made me proactive about updating plans and getting out there with my business in a much bigger way.

7. Realising I loved coaching and facilitating change in others. This was a monumental moment for me because until then my whole career had been about facilitating positive change for the bottom line of organisations. I loved making a difference, and in that moment it transferred from making a difference in companies to making a difference within the individual.

These events have all shaped my thinking and my view of the world. They have made me believe what is possible, and what isn't. Moments like this have reinforced my subconscious beliefs and fears about myself. They have also girded me to believe more in myself and my potential.

Your events will be different. How they have shaped your inner world will of course be different too. From the seven key events and thinking about how they have shaped my thinking, I discovered the following key themes about myself.

Step 3: My key themes:
- Need for financial security
- Fairness
- Adventure, variety
- Freedom and choice

- Autonomy
- Knowledge that I can make what I want to happen if I want it enough
- Making a difference
- Recognition for my work
- Passion for enabling others

My list gives me clarity about how I operate and a deeper understanding of why I am like I am. I know that I always have to feel like I am moving forward, making my own decisions and have an adventure or two planned... work or personal, that will stretch and challenge me. I also need the feedback and recognition that I am making a difference. And within all of that I know I am driven to make good money. Knowing this leads me to a greater acceptance of me. It also keeps me aware of how I need to create and manage my business to satisfy these drivers.

If I'm honest, at times I can feel conflicted about owning my own business when I have a strong need for financial security. I have learnt to reconcile that over the years by delving into my numbers, having a sales pipeline and always having savings to fall back on. The longer I have my own business, the more confident I am it will be okay.

What has come up for you from this exercise?

Reflecting on the exercise, consider these questions:

1. **How do you think it contributes to your situation now, either as an employee or a business owner?**

2. **How can you use these insights to help you?**

3. **What may you need to start doing differently to reconcile your conflicts?**

Why are you doing it?

When you are considering starting your own business, there is something you need to deeply consider.

Why?

An essential factor to consider is WHY you want to start your own business.

> Knowing the deep, real reason behind you starting the venture will help you stay focused, fuel your passion and determination, and lift you when you are feeling despondent and want to throw it all in.

What makes starting this new business worthwhile? Worth stopping what you are doing now; worth changing your life and your source of income; worth the long hours; worth having every waking thought consumed by the business; worth the stretch of your comfort zone? What will make this business really worth all of that for you (and possibly your family)?

Knowing deeply why you are starting the business and why you want it to be a success will give you a foundation of trust. Trust in yourself and your motivations. Trust in the reasons behind your decisions. And as importantly as you trusting yourself, when others know your motivation and deep reason why, they will start to trust you too. Trust is an essential building block for a business, whether it be trust in yourself or your potential customers having trust in you and what you say you will deliver. A transparent understanding of why you have the business will enable this to be built.

Chapter 3: Are YOU cut out for it?

Whatever that reason is, it must be compelling, motivating and aligned with your key drivers and values. Your reason why will underpin how you approach everything.

- How you start your business.
- The business plan you create.
- Whether or not you go for funding.
- Do you employ staff straight away?
- How much time you spend working every day
- Do you devote weekends to it?

At times, running your own business will move from the peaks of exhilaration to the troughs of frustration and everywhere in between. Be clear about the vision you wish to create, the impact you want to have and the difference it will make to you. This clarity of purpose will support you, inspire you and pull you through those dark moments.

Exercise: Why are you doing it?

Take some time and ask yourself these questions. Let your heart and your intuition guide your responses.

1. Why are you creating your business?
2. What is your driving reason that makes this business worth it?
3. What do you get from having this business?
   - Do you want to leave a legacy? Something that will affect thousands if not millions of people for generations to come?
   - Or is for freedom, flexibility and to have control over your life?
4. Are you passionate about what you want to create and how you want to use your expertise?

5. Do you want to spend time working on something you love, your passion, and make money from it?

I have seen many Corporate Crossovers recreate the same conditions they left behind in their last job: long working hours, working too hard, high stress. They lost sight of the purpose behind crossing over and, unknowingly, ended up in the same place.

Knowing why you created your business can help you make key decisions as you set it up.

A client of mine, Karen, was a new Corporate Crossover when we started working together. She had left a successful and long PR career to create her own consultancy. It would have been easy for her to recreate the life she left behind as she was well-networked and well-regarded. But her reason for crossing over was to have more time with her family, especially her daughter who was very ill. Because this was at the forefront of her reason to create her own business, we worked together for her to find a viable business framework that met all of her needs. High on her list of priorities was a defined set of working hours that she would be able to keep to; that would satisfy her clients but leave her energy for her personal life. She was able to enjoy professional success and still have time to devote to her daughter. Two years later, Karen is still delighted with the deliberate decisions she made early on.

4 What could you do?

So you've decided you want to leave. You are clear on your idea, confident about your ability to make it work and you are committed.

But wait! What if you don't have an idea?

You are totally committed to being self-employed, to having more freedom and flexibility over your time... But there is one tiny issue. What will your business be?

If you don't have an idea for your business but you are committed to leaving, make it your intention to be open-minded. Look for new opportunities around you. Start to deliberately question the status quo.

When you see an area that piques your interest, ask yourself:

- What if this were different?
- I wonder how else this could be done?

Your mind needs to be open to possibility if you are searching for 'that' idea.

> Having a clear business idea is the first step in the journey of the Corporate Crossover.

Clarity comes through clearly articulating what the business is, what you will be selling and to whom you are selling it.

41

Ideas for the business come from many places. It may be a chance conversation, an extension of the work you already do, a deeply held passion, or wanting to truly express your deepest values in a meaningful way. Ideas can start as a little flicker in the back of your mind and then grow into a tangible proposition. Or they leap out at you and take on a life of their own.

It is the toxic culture, the desire for more control over one's life and increased flexibility that fuels the idea and allows it to be birthed into the world. From the Corporate Crossovers survey of 300 women, only six per cent cited that they had a great idea or that they had always wanted to run their own businesses. It is not a driving idea, or the quest to be self-made millionaire entrepreneurs that causes these women to leave. They choose a different life.

Frustration, disappointment, a feeling you are worth more – all these add fertiliser to the seed of your ideas. The little thought that says, "I could be doing something else" grows into a green shoot, and then into something you can lean on. Ideas and opportunities start to become more evident once the seed is planted.

> As you allow an idea to grow, you gain confidence that it could replace your existing work and income source.

You start to imagine yourself running the business and your motivation is fuelled by externalising your thinking. You begin to talk to friends, family, partners and people you trust. Articulating your idea aloud and in some cases, defending it, will enable you to get clarity. Over time your idea develops into the start of a business.

From my research and the 50 in-depth interviews I conducted with successful Corporate Crossovers, there are four ways to create a business idea:

FOUR WAYS TO CREATE A BUSINESS IDEA

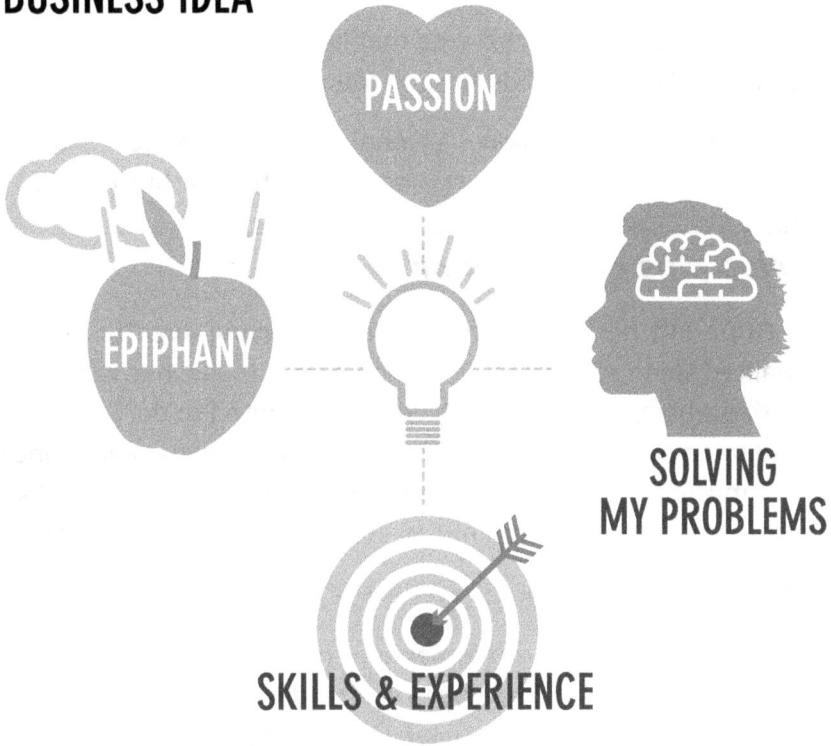

PASSION

EPIPHANY

SOLVING
MY PROBLEMS

SKILLS & EXPERIENCE

1. Follow your passion

When you are passionate about something, you find it easy to talk about. You love learning more about it, and you are happy to spend time thinking and being involved with activities related to that passion. Chances are you also have a great deal of knowledge about that subject.

An easy place to find an idea for your business is to consider what you are passionate about. Is it sailing, cooking, neuroscience or something else?

Are there things you used to be passionate about when you were younger? Perhaps in the course of being heavily involved in your career, or family, or both, this passion has dwindled and became dormant. Could you rekindle that flame of interest?

Or maybe it is a new-found area that lights you up, that sparks your energy and makes you feel happy and touches your potential?

Here are some fabulous examples of successful Corporate Crossovers who followed their passions to create their businesses.

Passion plus conversation

Galia Orme left her job as an internet marketing director knowing she wanted to do something that allowed her to live her values. She left without being sure of exactly what she wanted to do. She says, "I wanted to do something that I love. I've got two big passions. One of them is music and the other is chocolate." Knowing she was unlikely to earn any serious money in music, she chose her other passion.

After a series of serendipitous events she created CHOC Chick.

"I love chocolate. It just so happened, I met someone I hadn't seen in a long time. She had been very ill and she was gluten free, dairy free, she couldn't have any sugar in her diet. She'd gone on this course to learn how to make raw chocolate which is a much healthier way of making and eating chocolate.

When I tried it I just thought, 'My God, that's just like the chocolate we used to have when I was a child in South America.' I couldn't believe that it was so easy to make and so initially I was just making it for myself and my family. So, I thought, I'm going to try selling it. I set up the on-line business first, because I had that background. It just seemed like a natural thing to do."

Passion plus observation

Joanne Napier was a senior consultant at Cap Gemini. She also asked herself, "What do I love?" She considered what friends had commented on about her over the years. She says: "If I was to do something that I enjoy doing, I love to go shopping, you'll always find me pottering around home stores. I found my friends were saying to me, 'You've got nice taste, what colour do you think I should have?' I couldn't wait for the new home catalogue to come out from Laura Ashley and I thought, 'Why not try and do something with this?"

An astute observation whilst out shopping led to her business idea. "I saw me everywhere. I saw lots of women with babies walking around the shops at 10 o'clock on a Wednesday morning. I suddenly realised there's so many experienced, educated women out there that have made the decision to spend time with their family and therefore they have had to sacrifice everything else."

Joanne wanted to provide a platform for these women to earn money and still be home for their children. She also noticed there was a surge in social selling via home parties. So she combined her passion, her 'aha' moment about other mothers and a growing market trend and created Linen Loft, a social selling service that sells beautiful quality homewares via parties in customers' homes.

2. Solving your own problems

Many business ideas evolve from a need that the founder has. She needs a service or a product and realises it doesn't exist. Interestingly, the women that I spoke to saw the need when they entered a new lifestyle stage: parenthood. Conversations with other people like them supported the need for the idea and, voila, a business was born!

How often have you been frustrated by a product not performing as you had hoped, or wondered why someone hasn't created a particular gadget to make your life easier?

Or maybe you have already had that flash of inspiration when you were in the shower, creating a product to solve your problem, but you didn't do anything with it.

The benefit of creating a solution to your problem as the basis for your business idea is that you are intimately aware of the issues that you are trying to solve. There is a high probability that you will also know other people with the same problem, enabling you to get to an even greater understanding of the issue and how you will solve it successfully.

A problem plus a conversation

Wouldn't it be great if we could do something to suit our needs?" said Maria Johnson's husband, wanting a larger choice of activities for their two young children. "We didn't have anywhere to take the kids at weekend other than out in the park; there weren't any play centres." So the idea for Eddie Catz, a chain of indoor play centres for children was born.

A problem plus a gap in the market

A light bulb moment came to Sally Preston, founder of Babylicious, when talking with other mothers. As a mum she wanted to be able to feed her babies food that was healthy, nutritious and freshly-cooked with no nasties.

"We were lamenting about how we couldn't buy homemade food like we would make, that we would tirelessly place into ice cube trays and freeze. I thought, why can't I do it myself?" She decided to save herself and other mothers time by creating a range of freshly-made, pureed healthy meals for babies. Sally started the business from her dining room table. Key retailers also saw the gap in the market for her offering, and her business grew quickly. Since then she has diversified and grown the brand into Kiddylicious snacks – based on exactly the same principles –something she wanted to give her kids but couldn't find.

3. Leveraging your experience

Identifying the business idea that will fuel you to leave can also be based on doing what you are already doing. Continuing in your profession but instead of doing it for a corporation as a paid employee, doing it for yourself. You build on your experience and network to create a new business, as a freelancer, interim or consultant.

For many this can seem like the low risk option because you have the skills and experience required to make it a success. You may really love what you do but be disillusioned with the environment within which you are doing it.

Transplanting and repackaging your existing skills and experience is what many freelancers, consultants and interim professionals do.

You may have been in an industry which has equipped you with all the skills and knowledge you need to make the idea a success. Confidence and contacts are already established when you start your business using this approach. It is an effective way to quickly gain traction with your new business, giving you more quick wins to fuel your self-belief and business success.

Julie Anixter, Co-Founder and Executive Editor at Innovation Excellence, offers this advice for women who are creating a business leveraging their experience: "Get the company to hire you as a consultant before you leave. Think about building a bridge, because if they value you enough to hire you why wouldn't they do it again? Without doing anything unethical, turn to the people who know you best to help you start. Be authentic. Tell them what your dream is and let them support it. Go for it!"

Experience plus opportunity

Lucy Brazier, a publishing veteran of thirty years, now founder of Executive Secretary magazine: "Because I'd been in publishing, I'd always wanted to launch my own magazine. The magazine I now own used to be a newsletter. I had conversations with the owner over a long period of time. But I never had enough money to do the website properly or do the magazine the way I really wanted to. When I got my redundancy money, I knew that now I had the opportunity to do this. I never doubted at all that it was going to work."

Experience plus technology

Susan Moore, founder of Moore VA, a virtual assistance organisation, transitioned her experience as a senior executive assistant in large banks into the virtual world. "I had seen virtual assistance on my radar and I knew that technically as a personal assistant, or secretary, or executive assistant I could do it."

4. Epiphany

The Aha! moment. Elusive when we want one, abundant when we take a shower! That moment of clarity and insight culminating in a spark that you just know is the right idea for you to build your business on.

> If you are short of an idea and you feel that epiphanies elude you, it is time to freshen up your thinking.

The easiest way to get fresh thinking is to change the stimulus reaching your brain. Quite simply, it's about doing some things differently and trying new experiences.

Epiphanies happen as your brain churns through information. They can be triggered by new pieces of information that can unlock the solution to a problem that you have been churning through in the back of your mind.

How to freshen up your thinking!

If you commute to work, try taking a different route. Drive a new way, take a different bus or get off a stop early and walk longer. Simply changing your set routine means that you will no longer be on autopilot and you will have to focus on where you are and where you are going. Your brain will be more engaged and observant. You will see things you haven't seen before and then start to think different thoughts. It's the different thoughts that lead to an epiphany!

Likewise trying new experiences, a new class, a new restaurant, a new sport or hobby forces your brain to work in different ways. So not only are your experiences new activities but, again, you are making your brain work harder. As your brain takes in all this new information it has to input it into your long-term memory. Once it is in, your brain

49

will have fresh new stimulus to get to work on. It is when the brain makes sense of all the new information, that moment of insight, or epiphany, will come. Don't force it, just get out there and get stimulated!

Keep a notebook close to record your observations and ideas. Every week take some time out to reflect on your notes. Start to consider which ideas could be expanded upon for a business. What captures your imagination, makes you smile when you think about it? Which could you see yourself doing for the next five years?

Try not to censor any thought that you have. Write them down as they come, because you never know where that idea may lead.

5 Making the decision to leave

You have a good rating on the Corporate Crossover Quiz – If you haven't take the free quiz to see how ready you are to start your business, go to www.corporatecrossovers.com/quiz – indicating you have the potential to be a successful Corporate Crossover. You have clarity on your business idea. You are fed up with your work environment. You spend more time dreaming of your new life than working. You have started to tell people you are leaving.

But, twelve months later, you are still there. Still in your office, still in the same job, still frustrated. You have a strong yearning to leave, yet you stay.

My research shows that it's common to weigh up the 'Stay or go?' equation for some time. Levels of frustration and stress may be increasing – but still you remain. What is it that makes women continue where they are, even if they know they want to leave and they have a business idea? What keeps them locked in this corporate prison, living a life that doesn't resonate anymore?

You probably feel trapped by one or more of these factors:

- Fear
- Income
- Security
- Status

Whilst your comfort zone is no longer very comfortable, remaining in your job appears to be the easiest option. Day after day you endure it. Boring your friends with your stories of stress, evil bosses, ridiculous decisions and how your talents are wasted.

Why do you stay?

Years ago, I worked for a very well-known global technology company. Early on in my time there, I was given the project of redesigning the channel to market, making our products more accessible for consumers, leveraging the brand and increasing our profit margins. The existing reseller base was livid, concerned about the impact to its sales and livelihood. At the time I didn't realise that I had been given the poisoned chalice, so enamoured was I with the company's brand, my title, my increased salary and my lovely European company car. No-one in the company supported this move as we came closer to announcing it at the channel conference and commencing the pilot. Determinedly, I pushed on, not reading the signals and especially not listening to my body. My health started to deteriorate, I developed flu symptoms that never disappeared, huge cold-sores on my lips and I piled on the pounds as I drank more and more to cope with going back to work the next day. Friends told me to leave and I hated everything about my job, yet I stayed.

A year later and working in an international position for the company, my role was made redundant as part of the global work force shrinking by 15%. I realise now that being forced out was the only way I would have left that company.

Looking back on this now, it seems crazy. Why would an intelligent woman do this to herself? For me, it was blind determination, the belief that things would improve and an identity that was intimately entwined with my job. I had no time or energy to even consider other options. I also had a false belief that all workplaces were ultimately like this, so I might as well stick it out.

Chapter 5: Making the decision to leave

I'm not the only one. Trisha Proud says she was unhappy for three years before she left – a long time to be miserable in your job. But she believed she had the power to change it, and tried to make her own niche in the company as happy and positive as she could. Only after trying that strategy for three years, yet still being unhappy, did she make the move.

After spending many years of your adult life in a certain pattern, enjoying a relatively secure level of income it can be hard to walk away. We may not realise how entangled our self-identity has become with what we do. Walking away from that can be scary and since it is the job of our subconscious to protect us, protect us it will. This is why it seems easier to stay than go. Rather than taking the leap to a new world, our subconscious will feed us with many reasons about why to stay. Your brain will feed you with statements of protection such as, "this is not the right time", "what a risky move it may be" and, "how could I ever succeed in business by myself?"

Thinking about making the move can cause us to become very self-critical, feeding our self-doubt and increasing our hesitancy to leave.

A research respondent who has been thinking of leaving for two years identifies all of her fears which make her stay in her job: "I am worried about my credibility – who will hire me? I fear getting bogged down in the administration of it all and then not being able to do what I set out to do. I also fear my own perfectionist/workaholic tendencies might know no bounds."

Fears can also appear as doubts about whether or not we will be good enough. Fear about getting enough clients, fear of not knowing what I need to know. In some cases these fears are real, but most often they are doubts, trying to keep us safe. But there are also those elements which we are highly conscious of that make us stay.

Fear

Fear paralyses you.

It keeps you stuck in one place, wondering, "What if?"

What are you afraid of? For most people it's the fear of failure, fear of not making a living, fear of having to run a business, the fear of stepping out of the corporate confines and the fear of risking your current level of relative comfort.

Fear is the number one reason that stuck entrepreneurial women gave me when I asked them why they stayed in their jobs. One respondent summed it up: "Fear of the unknown, capital constraints, not having the confidence quite yet to do it, fear of not being good enough, of not having enough money to survive. And what will people say?"

Not all of us manage to articulate our fears quite that precisely. Often we make these fears sound more valid by covering them up with reasons that are hard to argue with: "There's a recession", "I need to do more research," "The economy isn't right for my idea at the moment."

These excuses stop you from taking the time to examine your business idea, to create a business plan and analyse the viability of your proposition. Some of the women I spoke to stop themselves before they even start.

These blanket excuses stop us from acting and prevent us from examining and, therefore, overcoming our deepest fears.

Chapter 5: Making the decision to leave

But there is *no risk* whatsoever in:

- Dreaming
- Articulating your idea onto paper
- Conducting market research among friends and family
- Drafting potential cash flow spreadsheets
- Creating a business plan

Fear will always hamper you. Deciding to leave and acting on that decision takes confidence and fortitude.

Income

Money, money and more money. Golden handcuffs.

Like it or not, most of us spend what we earn.

Over the years of promotions and salary increases, your lifestyle comfortably expands to suck up most of your income. Walking away from this perceived financial security is very difficult. And it's even more difficult if you are the main breadwinner and have dependents.

> "What keeps me in my job? Money! And cowardice," admitted one survey respondent. I earn a lot in my corporate job and I'm worried I won't be able to increase my earnings from my own business. But mainly it is just that I'm a big fat coward and risk-averse, which means it is extra difficult for me to make the leap to doing this full time."

Research I conducted amongst women that are yet to crossover showed that the need for financial security is the key reason they stay. Even though they want to go, they dislike the toxic culture and they have a business idea, they remain stuck in their job. They will comment, "I'll leave my job as soon as I have more financial security," and "I have worked so hard to get where I am, it seems crazy to risk it all," and "I would definitely do it, if it weren't for my mortgage."

Before women leave their jobs, they want to have the confidence that their business idea will provide them with the same level of income they currently have. That's not likely, especially at first. But not all of life's rewards are financial, and it's impossible to quantify the benefits of being your own boss.

Security

If you started in your profession early in your working life, it can be hard to let go of the idea that this is your whole world, and the only world where you can succeed. It may be that you have been in your profession for many years and only utilised a narrow set of skills, albeit deeply.

> You may feel ill-equipped to start a business. Instead of analysing what your skills gaps may be, you stay.

You may have invested years of your life in this career and organisation. You may think you are on the fast track of career success. You may have been identified as "high potential". You may be thinking, "I have been working here for so long, I know I'll be made partner (or managing director or senior vice president) soon. It's worth hanging out until then."

But many of the Corporate Crossovers I interviewed would tell you otherwise. They would say that the risks are worth it. There's a different kind of security that comes from running your own business – you can't be made redundant or fired, and you can choose your own destiny.

Chapter 5: Making the decision to leave

Gwyn Cready was with the pharmaceutical company GlaxoSmithKline for 20 years. When her business unit was relocated to a different city, she decided to take the redundancy that was offered and pursue her dream of becoming an author. She says, "I never would have left GSK unless they told me my job was moving. Now I meet with my friends who are still in a thankless corporate job and they make a lot of money but they look like they're dead inside. I say, "Maybe you should become a teacher." And their faces would light up and they'd say, "Oh God, I would love to teach but I could not afford to live like that." I keep saying, "Believe me, you will make less money but you will be so much happier and you will never go back." They look at me like I am offering heroin, as if I am trying to draw them into a dangerous thing."

Status

Let's not forget the social status of working for certain organisations. Most of us are good employees who feel great pride for our organisation. In some cases, the strength of the company culture makes us think that we are privileged to have this job, with this company. Other people will tell you, or you will tell yourself, that walking away from this senior position would be a terrible mistake.

> The money you earn contributes to your status, and helps you keep up with your peers.

To leave your job would be to put yourself on a different level to your former colleagues. This can feel like a demotion, although it doesn't need to.

One of my interviewees said: "I have a girlfriend who is a lawyer in a big practice, and if she was being honest, she would say to you, 'Why did I do all of this? I'd really rather be running a birthday party events company. But she realises she's bought into the lifestyle being a lawyer gives her."

You will be challenging others' assumptions about the role of work in their lives.

The fear of "What will people think?" is another status issue. None of us want our friends and family to think poorly of our decisions or to have our status lowered in their eyes. Your partner may be more attached to your income and status than you are, and perhaps doesn't want to see it change. Your fellow workmates could feel abandoned and resentful if you decided to jump ship – they would rather see you hanging about, luxuriating in the misery with them.

How to feel confident in your decision to leave

Getting confidence about leaving and starting your business is the second part the crossover journey.

Not only do you need to have confidence about starting your business but confidence about your decision to leave life as an employee.

Why would you leave that perceived security and support of the corporate environment? The thing I know from my own experience and that of clients is that we always look back on our past corporate life with rose-tinted glasses. It seems more enjoyable in hindsight than it was at the time.

Chapter 5: Making the decision to leave

Be clear on exactly why you are leaving your corporate job and corporate life. If you have taken redundancy, think about why you have chosen not to search for another employed position.

Complete the following two exercises to increase your confidence about your decision. They will also support you when you feel like you may have made a wrong decision. If this does happen, revisit these exercises and remember why you made the right decision at that time.

When we need to make a decision, a really big decision with significant implications, we can feel so wrought by the confusion and lose our perspective. We become myopic and our thinking narrows. It is easy to remain stuck.

Exercise: A letter to myself – Sliding Doors

This exercise allows you to imagine what life could be like in five years' time, depending on what decision you make. By thinking five years into the future, you loosen your grip on the current reality and your perspective shifts. This will help you make a cleaner decision away from the frenzy of the moment.

> You can download the worksheet to accompany this exercise at www.corporatecrossovers.com/when-its-time

Write yourself a letter entitled *'Sliding Doors – Path A Versus Path B'*. You will create two stories of your life, each one dependent on the decision you could take now.

Path A:

Write a story of what your life will be like in five years if you stay in your job, remaining in corporate life.

Path B:

Then write another story of what your life will be like in five years if you leave your job now and start your own business.

In both stories, be as detailed as possible. Describe clearly what your typical day and week would be like for each option five years into the future. Imagine the sort of work you will be doing, who you will be interacting with, what decisions you will be making, the types of products and services you will be involved with. Consider how much money you will be earning.

Also think about what your personal life will be like in both scenarios. What hours will you be working? How much free time will you have? What will your stress levels be like? Who will you be spending time with. Who will you be learning from? What holidays will you have?

Once you have completed each story, reflect on them. Ensure you are being honest. What do you think and feel about the different scenarios that you have created? Is there anything you would change?

From the two letters, which five year outcome appeals the most to you? Why?

It may be that you write these letters, leave them and then revisit them over a number of days and weeks. You may need time to contemplate the different outcomes. This is a big decision and once you start to ponder the choices and different paths you could go down, more thoughts and ideas will naturally float up.

I love this exercise as it gives you the rare opportunity to actively design and take control of your life and become the architect of your own destiny.

Chapter 5: Making the decision to leave

Exercise: For and against Lists

A more objective exercise is to write a list of the benefits and costs of each option.

You can download the worksheet to accompany this exercise at www.corporatecrossovers.com/when-its-time

A list of 'Stay in my job' and a second list of 'Start my own business'.

Write a for and against list for both options, staying in employment and creating your own business. Even if you have already left and need reinforcement that this was the right decision, this can also be a useful exercise to do retrospectively. I know from experience this helped me to cement my commitment to staying self-employed.

To help with this, consider the following topics when writing your lists. You will of course have some of your own criteria as well:

- Income
- Colleagues
- Time
- Responsibility
- Support
- Flexibility
- Happiness
- Holidays
- Potential
- Satisfaction
- Freedom
- Fulfilling a dream

- Living in purpose
- Fun
- Stress
- Commute
- Fear
- Challenge
- Adventure
- Cash flow
- Security
- Travel
- Control

Once you have done these lists, put them away for a day or two and revisit with a fresh mind. What comes up for you when you see it? Do you feel more confident about your decision to leave? If not, consider what might be blocking you from clarity, and take some time to break it down into its smaller components. By doing this, it will be easier for you to solve.

6 Getting ready to cross over

Our minds can talk us out of taking the bold steps to get our business moving. Isolation can have us dreaming of the ready-made network of work colleagues that we once enjoyed. As one new Corporate Crossover says, "The mental battle with oneself is hard! From issues with confidence, time management, motivation, believing in yourself... It can be a lonely ride!"

> Doubt, fear and isolation are potentially crippling to a fledgling business owner.

This is a terrible thing to admit but when I was employed in my corporate job, I didn't have a network. Not one that stretched beyond the organisational chart. If you weren't on that chart, I probably didn't know you.

Looking back, I can't believe how myopic and insular I was. With the benefit of hindsight I now see I missed a big opportunity to meet a wide range of people, who even back then, I could have learnt from and been inspired by. I know had I done that, my network would have not only been bigger but it would have a different quality to it. Upon leaving my job, I would have found more business faster. I would have also had a richer range of experience and talent to draw on and help me as I went through the different phases of my business journey.

Getting ready exercise: Establish your wider network

Who do you know that you would like to be connected with in the future? Think about colleagues, past and present, people you meet at conferences, events, networking meetings. Ensure that you connect with them. Linked In is an effective tool to manage and track your network.

> Take the time now to establish and strengthen your wider network of contacts and connections.

From your wider network you can start to identify who your mini-support team could be as you go through these transition phases?

- Who can you talk to about your fears, your concerns and also your wins, hopes and dreams?
- Who will remind you of the reasons that you left and decided on this path?
- Who will be honest with you?

Getting ready exercise: Create your list of cheerleaders

Change not only of your work, but also your identity, support network and even your confidence levels.

> Crossing over is a significant decision and represents a period of high change.

As you get ready to crossover, take time to identify your cheerleaders. These will be people who you trust and that you know will be honest with you. They will see your potential and that of your business. Like cheerleaders, they will lift your spirits when you need support and also celebrate your successes with you.

Give some thought to the type of support you will need.

- Who is in your network that will support you and your plans?
- Who would you like to have close to celebrate your successes and to support you during your low moments?

They may be friends who have their own businesses, people you have met on training courses if you retrained, a business coach, other people at your networking group or even your accountant, lawyer or designer.

Once you have your list, reach out to them. Tell them what you are planning and ask for their support. Most people will be honoured to be asked and will gladly encourage you as you cross over. You only have to ask.

Getting ready exercise: Identify your networking groups

Everyone I have spoken to about what has helped them has mentioned their network – people they have known for a while, or recently met. The networks enable them to feel connected, replacing that social loss of the office. They can also provide stimulation, advice and even new business opportunities.

> If you don't have a rich, diverse network,
> start to create one.

Ponder the people you have interacted with over the years and start to reconnect with them. There are many ready-made business network groups out there designed for business owners. They range in the amount of structure they have, focus on business building versus connecting, industry specialties and whether they are women only or mixed. Networks can be physical and also virtual. Many great networks exist on line with active forums and an amazing exchange of ideas across the world.

You may not find the one that fits you best straightaway but keep looking. Over time you will come to relish the meetings as these strangers become your friends. Your issues and problems will become normalised by meeting with other business owners who may be going through the same issue or have been through it already and can offer advice. They can be wonderful places to share successes, and even make long lasting friendships and business partnerships.

Before you leave your job, do some research on local business networks. It is as simple as Googling "Business networking groups". Create a shortlist of 10 and start trying them out. It is important to visit them as some will suit you, others won't. Have an open mind. You may choose to meet some of the members for coffee. Ask them what they love about that networking group, and how it has benefited their business. You may also want to ask them if they feel it has been a good investment of their time and money for their business.

Different approaches to transitioning

Leaving your job to create the business and life of your dreams can sound easy to implement in a book. The reality for many women is that they are the sole breadwinner (or their financial contribution to the household is essential), so leaving their job without financial security is untenable. The 'should I stay or go?' equation that goes on in their head must include the calculation of making this work financially and the level of risk they are willing to bear.

What then? How do these women make it work? There are different approaches to the transition. They develop the business plan in the evenings after work, or they drop a day a week in their current job to dedicate to the start up. Some leave their current employment to start contracting and to learn about a new business model. The transition stage is varied and fits with that individual's readiness, attitude to risk and sense of urgency.

Gradual entry

If you are risk-averse, a gradual entry can be the best option for you. Whilst you have the security of an income, you can start to assess the opportunity for your business idea and, in some cases, start it. Use the time to research, test the idea and assess its viability. Over this time your confidence and experience will also grow.

> Maria Johnson, founder of Eddie Catz, took a long-term approach to her transition: "I dropped one day a week of my job and started to write the business plan. For the last year of my corporate working life, as well as having a baby, I started to put together a business plan for Eddie Catz. Once the plan was complete I quit my job to focus on lining up the financing. My husband and I gave ourselves one year. We agreed that if we couldn't raise the finance in a year, I would have to go back and get a job."

> Finances can determine the speed of the transition. Whilst Jo Lindsay, of Lindsay Interiors, formerly a Senior IT Manager, had started her business and been trading for over a year, she still decided to take a gradual transition into the business. She wanted to reinvest all profit into building up stock and marketing. Unfortunately she had to leave her job early. She says: "It was quite difficult because I wasn't quite ready to leave my job when I did; the situation was a little bit forced. I wasn't taking any money out of the business at the time. I went from earning a very good salary to nothing overnight. I panicked and thought, 'Right, I'm going to have to get a temp job just doing general admin work for a bit.' That lasted for about five months."

Contracting and consulting

The idea for the new business can be a continuation of what we do already in our roles, except that now we want to do it for ourselves. Working in a large corporate with an established framework of operation can leave one unprepared for the realities of creating and managing a small business.

> Working inside a business similar to the one you wish to create allows you to experience what you are getting into from the inside out.

You learn about the mechanics of the business and you are getting paid. You build up a different network of contacts and expand your thinking and your world. This leads to increased confidence and a better understanding of what you are about to embark on.

Laura Bergerson, founder of Channel Impact and Talent Impact, realised that when she left the corporate world she wanted to continue the type of work she was doing there. "I left my job and I thought, 'Well, if I'm going to do channel consulting I guess I should go work for a channel consultancy as an independent contractor.' I did that for about two years. I used the name Bergerson Group, I subbed through them and I got exposed to how to run a consulting practice. I'd never been on that side of the business. I really got to learn the business."

Utilising maternity leave

For others, maternity leave can create the space needed to incubate something else.

Chapter 6: Getting ready to cross over

Zoe Sinclair had her business idea, for helping parents and employees achieve work-life balance through seminars, when she first returned to work after the birth of her first child.

"Eighteen months back at work passed very quickly and I was pregnant again. While on my second maternity leave I took the time to work up my business idea." Not long after the birth of her second child, Employees Matter was also born.

What will work be like for you?

When you are getting ready to go, it is crucial to fully consider exactly what you are going to do.

Transitioning from the framework of your job – the structure and the boundaries it provides – is challenging. When you leave your job, you have to recreate this structure and framework yourself. Not only in terms of how you structure your time, but also how you create a new role for yourself.

As employees, most of us go to the office to work. We are defined as a working person. People have certain expectations of what we do and when we do it; when we are available and when we are not. There is an expectation around how much free time we have in the evenings and weekends. These boundaries are magically defined for us because we are working in an organisation. Leave this and start working for yourself, and you will suddenly see those boundaries disappear – for yourself and for others.

> How will you value yourself and your time when you are self-employed? What value will you give your role?

Your perceived availability, or not, is defined by setting your boundaries and a structure for your day. This in turn means you must get very clear on what your value is. What is your role now you have left your corporate job?

Is creating and building a successful and profitable big business your key focus? Or are you building it in between the school run and other responsibilities? How do you talk about what you are doing now you have left the corporate world?

Defining your role and knowing clearly what value you are creating allows you to create boundaries with others and be assertive in pushing back when you feel people are encroaching on your valuable time, energy and space. Just because you have left paid employment doesn't mean you aren't working anymore and can take up the extra household tasks.

> The trap that many Corporate Crossovers fall into is not valuing their time and business as much as they did when they worked for an employer.

How you value yourself and your business will be reflected in how others value you. This is critical to the ultimate success or failure of your business.

You will go through a significant transition and you will need to reshape your view of yourself. Others will need to as well. Whether it be a partner, spouse, children, friends or parents, they need to understand and support that you are still working.

As a Corporate Crossover comments: "Working from home, it was very difficult to set the expectations. To everyone else it was like I was just at home. So people visiting had no regard that I was actually working during the day.

Chapter 6: Getting ready to cross over

After the initial enthusiasm has waned it can be easy to use others' expectations of us to fall into a pattern that will not support the growth of the business. In other words, it's more fun to have coffee with your friends who drop in, but if you fall into these traps you'll never run a successful company.

Starting and growing a business requires you to put yourself out there and to frequently step out of your comfort zone. If we have people who would prefer us to be around for them and to help them more than help us, it can be easy to let those moments pass and we find that a year later the business is actually an expensive hobby instead of a proper business venture.

Exercise: Get a clear idea of your value by creating a job description

You can download the worksheet to accompany this exercise at www.corporatecrossovers.com/when-its-time

Chances are that in your employed role you had a job description.

Job descriptions are designed to clearly outline:

- your role
- your objectives
- what your contribution to the organisation is
- your responsibilities and your tasks

When you were asked what you did, your job description was the formal and detailed explanation.

In your own business, you are working, you have a job. Do you have a job description? Or do you just do it all?

Creating your job description for your role in your new business will help you:

- get clear about your value
- easily see what contribution you make to the business
- recognise all that you do
- clearly articulate exactly what you are doing now

When you see the value in yourself, others will too.

This will be the catalyst to enable you to easily create boundaries around your time and energy to ensure that you have the space to work effectively on your business.

In your business, wearing many hats, you deal with whatever comes up, whether you have expertise in it or not. You spend precious time in areas that you know little about or have no natural aptitude for. Yet because it's your own business, you do it anyway.

By creating your job description, you can start to clarify the value you bring to the business. If you ever feel overwhelmed, completing this exercise may help you to identify the specific areas in which you need to get additional resources.

Here is a simple way to do a job description:

1. My title
2. What do I love to do?
3. How will I bring value to the business?
4. What will I be responsible for?
5. What attributes do I need to be successful in this role?

Let me give you an example. Kate is an author and trainer who specialises in training landlords to help them have success with their rental properties. If she were to do the job description exercise, then this is what she would create.

Kate's example:

1. **My title**

   Author and trainer

2. **What do I love to do?**

   Help landlords sleep better at night by giving them all the information they need to run their tenancies successfully. I love providing them with the right information via my book, my website and in my workshops.

3. **How do I bring value to the business?**

   - By creating content for books to sell
   - By designing and leading workshops that landlords pay to attend
   - By actively commenting on rental issues in media

4. **What am I responsible for?**

   - The overall success of the business, driving sales of my book and registrations to my workshops
   - The production and delivery of content
   - Managing the brand, income, expenses and cashflow

5. **What attributes do I need to be successful in this role?**

   - Detailed knowledge of tenancy legislation
   - Experience in the industry
   - Passion about working with landlords to help them improve
   - Great written and verbal communication skills

So, there is Kate's *ideal* job description. As a one-woman enterprise, she also has to wear many other hats. By also creating additional job descriptions for the other roles her business needs to operate successfully, she can be clear about which hat she is wearing when and thus reduce feeling overwhelmed. This will help her understand that it is just part of the business she needs to run at that moment in time.

By creating these simple job descriptions for all aspects of your business, you can decide which job you are doing when. By realising the value that you are adding by completing that specific task, you will feel happier about doing it. The added bonus of completing this exercise early on in your business is that when you do come to expand and acquire additional resources, staff or outsourced, you will have a clear idea of what experience and expertise you need to support your growth.

Now you have created your job description, what do you think? Is it a job that you would relish, be excited by and be eager to get going every morning? Or is it not exciting enough for you to fuel your flames to cross over?

7 Sorting out the finances

From my research, I discovered that the number one concern for the women considering leaving their corporate jobs to start their own business is money. Will you make the same level of income as you have now, less, or even more? It's not only the amount of money but also the cash flow – how regular and reliable will your income be?

> To feel financially secure about crossing over, make sure you have at least eight months' worth of savings to fall back on in case your business does not go according to plan.

Having enough savings to cover eight months of living expenses means that you can focus on making your business idea a success and not have the constant worry about covering your personal costs.

It may be that when you start the business, you are not the main or sole breadwinner for your family unit. Whatever your circumstances, it is still critical you do this, as life can change quite suddenly, and you may end up with these responsibilities.

One of my clients was in tears in our session as she was extremely worried about short-term revenue generation and cash flow for her business. Through her tears she said, "You know, when I started this, I was married and my husband provided for us. Now I'm divorced and have to make this business provide for me and my daughter."

So we went back to her marketing plans to drive sales, and we restructured the outgoings to give her a bigger safety net while her marketing activities gained traction and the business generated additional revenue. Between us we were able to find ways to make the business produce more cash. She was delighted to be able to draw down some extra income, and the strategies have also helped to drive sales since then.

How much do you need to live on?

If you don't have a budget for your living expenses create one now. Be realistic about what you actually spend every month. Do you want to keep spending at this level? Or can you cut back while you are in the start-up phase of the business?

Create this budget while you are still working and live by it. In this way, when you make the move from employment to your business, your lifestyle and spending patterns will not have to be another factor you need to adjust. You will have done the work already.

Looking at your finances now will get you into good habits for proactively managing the finances of your business.

Remember: information is power. Fully understanding your financial activity and situation will empower you as you cross over.

Exercise: Get financially focused

You can download the worksheet to accompany this exercise at www.corporatecrossovers.com/when-its-time

Chapter 7: Sorting out the finances

1. Create a budget for your day-to-day living expenses. Include rent or mortgage payments, food, utilities, car expenses, fuel, communication charges, public transport costs, gifts, clothing, travel, groceries, vacations and everything else.

2. Assess whether you have eight months' worth of living expenses saved.

3. Forecast how much money you will make in your business and how long it will take you to turn a profit. The further you are along in the business planning, the greater your accuracy and confidence will be.

Feeling confident about how the numbers work before you leave your job will make a huge difference to how you create and run your business. Understanding the finances of the business is critical, and if you don't know the difference between a profit and loss statement and cash flow – get help now!

Instead of shying away from the numbers, you need to embrace them and understand how the business is performing. Knowledge of the numbers will give you insights about what you need to focus on to grow your business and your profits.

> "I do all my accounts," says Galia Orme of CHOC Chick. "I have a really clear idea of what the outgoings are and what I need. I do weekly liabilities reports, what's coming in, what's going out. So I know. Beforehand I didn't think I was very good at maths; numbers have always frightened me. Now I do all the accounts and go through everything myself. I'm determined to make sure I know the financial state of the business all the time. It gives me confidence and I feel on top of the business. It's really important for me. It wasn't a skill I had before, or something I thought I was capable of doing."

How much could your business make?

A key question you will be asking yourself is, 'Will my business make any money?" Knowing the answer to this is a key part of your decision making process as you crossover. Prior to embarking on a complete business plan, I recommend that you start with some estimates to gain an initial sense of the financial potential of the business. Once you have made your decision to crossover, you will need to do full financial estimates, including a profit and loss statement and a cash flow forecast. There is more on this later on in the book.

Exercise: Back of the envelope profit and loss statement

You can download the worksheet to accompany this exercise at www.corporatecrossovers.com/when-its-time

If you are right at the start of your business planning, then a "back of the envelope" calculation can give you some indication of how viable your idea is. Warning: This does not replace a comprehensive profit and loss forecast with all running costs of your business. You will need to do one, but later. For now, start with initial estimates, until you get more information, quotes and understanding of how attractive your idea is to your ideal prospect.

1. **How many units do you want to sell?**

    Units could be product items or service hours.

2. **How much will you sell each item (or hour) for?**

    Estimate your selling price of each unit.

    Answer 1 x Answer 2 = Turnover or Revenue or Gross Sales

Chapter 7: Sorting out the finances

What do you think of the gross sales number? Does it look reasonable to you, or too small? Or maybe too large? Play with it, create different scenarios.

Once you have established the volume and price equation to generate your desired turnover, you also need to check if you will make a profit!

3. **How much will each unit cost to produce? (An estimate is fine here.)**

   Is this more or less than the price you wish to sell it at? Multiply the cost of each unit by the number you wish to sell (answer to question 1) to calculate your total cost of goods.

   Answer 1 x Answer 3 = Total Cost of Goods

4. **Estimate of Gross Profit**

   - Turnover - Total cost of goods = Gross profit.
   - This figure does not include any expenses of running the business, investing in capital, marketing, staff, insurances, taxes, etc. but at this early stage it will give an indication of what volume and price you needto set to make a profit before costs.

Back of the envelope profit and loss statement

Even at the most exploratory stages of business planning you must make the time for this simple 'back of the envelope' profit and loss statement. If there is no profit to be made (even at this stage of zero operating costs being allocated) then there is no point in pursuing the idea further. Unless you change the parameters to sell at a higher price or produce at a lower cost.

This is a very basic P&L (profit and loss). Understanding the sale price, costs and profit at the early stages of planning will all bolster your confidence about leaving.

Sales/Revenue		
Box 1	How many products or services will you sell in a year (or how many hours will you charge out)?	
Box 2	What will be the price each one sells at. (or what will be your fee per hour)?	
Total Revenue (Box A)	Box 1 multiplied by Box 2	£/$
Cost of Goods		
Box 3	Cost of buying or making the sold stock per unit/or cost of an hour	£/$
Box 1	How many products or services will you sell in a year (or how many hours will you charge out)?	£/$
Total Cost of Goods (Box B)	Box 1 multiplied by Box 3	£/$
Gross Profit (Box A – Box B)		£/$

Also, consider how long it will take you to make your first sale. It is unlikely you will make a sale immediately, and you need to factor in the time to produce the product or service, find prospects, sell, then close the sale, and issue your first invoice.

Exercise: How long until my first sale?

You can download the worksheet to accompany this exercise at www.corporatecrossovers.com/when-its-time

Chapter 7: Sorting out the finances

Activity	Time before sale
First Sale!	**0**

Sample answer below for online gift basket company:

Activity	Time before sale
Build website	Minus 12 weeks from sale
Get feedback and refine	Minus 10 weeks from sale
Source items for baskets	Minus 10 weeks from sale

Take photos of prototypes	Minus 8 weeks from sale
Start public relations	0 weeks
Start social media campaign	0 weeks
Site visitor buys	0 weeks – SALE!
Receive payment from customer	Immediately after sale

How do the numbers stack up?

Now you have three pieces of key information:

1. How much money you need to live on each month
2. A ballpark estimate of your business financials
3. How long it will take you to make a sale and earn money

These are very broad estimates but they will provide you with a good start for a more detailed financial planning and analysis which will be completed in your business plan.

Finding financial support

If you need to increase your understanding of business finance, there are many resources available. Try your bank; banks often have free courses and information on their websites. And if *your* bank doesn't have it, try one of its competitors. Ask around from other business owners where they discovered information, find a proactive accountant who speaks in your language, a tax advisor and a book keeper. You can always go to the library – you would be amazed at the number of business and finance books available.

Chapter 7: Sorting out the finances

Financial support can also extend to getting funding for the business. If you require capital to get your business off the ground, or ongoing funding as your business develops, you will have to acquire this. There are many types of financing available and what is best for you and your business will depend on your current circumstances, risk profile, and business requirements and projections.

There are four main financing options: equity, debt, sales and asset financing. With the exception of equity, they will mean that the business will take in borrowings. It is imperative that you get trustworthy advice in this arena. It may be that you consult with several experts before you form an opinion about which options are best for you.

Often Corporate Crossovers will shy away from examining the numbers. If you're the kind of person who tries not to look at her credit card statement in case it's too high, or avoids checking her bank balance if you know you're not going to like what you see, you'll need to change your ways.

> Without financial goals or progress reviews, you don't have a business. You have an expensive hobby.

It may be that you are fed up with being driven by spreadsheets at your corporate job, or you're "not a numbers person". We can get so busy in the day-to-day running of the business, it is easy to forget how far we have come and how much we have actually achieved. Once one day finishes, we lurch quickly into the next one. Get into the habit of reviewing what you have done daily, weekly and monthly.

Tracking your progress

It is important to track the financial progress of your business frequently. By reviewing the numbers regularly, you can make corrections to your levels of activity, your marketing direction and your expenditure, in order to get back on track with the goals of your business.

And it's not just the revenue, expenditure, profit and loss you need to track. Other milestones can be marketing targets, number of customers acquired and money spent. Milestones are critical to ensure you review your business frequently and that you are on top of the numbers. You must celebrate when you achieve them! This will bolster your feeling of success and increase your confidence that you have made the right decision.

> Julie Anixter says that managing the bottom line is the hard part of running your own business: "Being responsible, being the one who makes it happen or doesn't." She says that for her, business success is measured in numbers, and her companies will only be successful in her mind, "when the financial results reach a certain level."

Action: Weekly review

Every week, set up a regular meeting with yourself to review the business and the milestones you created in your business planning. That meeting should allow you to:

- Examine the financial health of the business, your sales achieved and the sales pipeline.
- Assess your marketing activity and ask, "Is it giving me the return I require?"
- Always ask, "Am I on target to meet my goals?"

A weekly review will keep you focused on your business goals, your priorities and also help you assess how far you have come and what else you need to prioritise.

8 The transition to being a Corporate Crossover

When you leave your job, willingly or not, you will go through a grieving process brought on by the change. Leaving a world you have known for many years and stepping out by yourself is a massive transition. You are leaving behind the familiar. You have said your goodbyes to the people you worked with. You need to say farewell to your way of life, your view of yourself in that role and the norms and conventions you have lived by – whether you liked them or not.

Travelling through the Corporate Crossover Transition Curve is expedited by being very clear about why you are undergoing this change. Holding onto that reason for creating this business and leaving your corporate job is key. What are the reasons for doing this? What are the benefits of making this change? How will your life be better?

If you didn't complete the previous exercise in Chapter 3 about the big reason why you are creating your own business, do it now! That way, when you go through a wobbly patch, you can reconnect with that reason. This will help you hold your course, and open you up to the possibilities and potential of your business once more.

The Corporate Crossover's Transition Model

Using Elizabeth Kubler-Ross's[1] five stages of grief model as a template, I have developed the Corporate Crossover Transition Model. This model has proved reassuring to many of my clients as they move through the ups and downs of a start-up business.

There are seven phases in the Corporate Crossover Transition Model. From my own experience and that of my clients, everyone goes through this model at a different pace. Some phases are more extreme than others, and in some you may linger longer. You may even travel back through phases – the model is not a one-way street. Events may occur that cause you to take a step back to a previous phase. Don't worry, this is normal.

What will make your transition unique? Your natural temperament, your reason for setting up the business, the amount and depth of preparation you have done, and your financial safety net.

THE CORPORATE CROSSOVERS TRANSITION MODEL

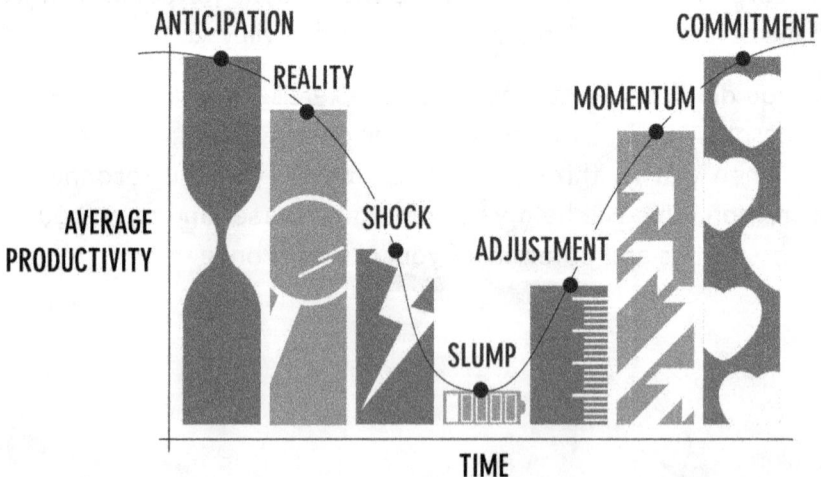

[1] Elizabeth Kubler-Ross On Death and Dying, Published by Scribner 1969
[2] Kessler, R. C., Turner, J.B., & House, J. S. (1988). The effects of unemployment on
86

Phase 1: Anticipation

You decide to leave and create your own business, or maybe you have taken redundancy and decided to start up your own venture. You feel hopeful, optimistic that it will all work out fine.

> You've crossed over and you feel liberated
> and empowered!

Often the excitement and relief felt at this stage is the energetic release that you are finally on your way, after thinking about it for so long.

Maria Johnson of Eddie Catz recalls her leaving moment: "The day I resigned I think my boss was stupefied. He could not believe i was leaving a well paid high flying position. I actually felt quite a sense of relief. It was scary. It took courage – I was with my company for over a decade – but it was satisfying. I felt free, which was lovely."

As the days and weeks go by, your optimism and eager anticipation start to fade. As you get into your new way of working with your new routines you start to realise what you have left behind. Confusion, doubt and worry start to erode your confidence. Doubt sets in: "Have I really made the right decision?" and "Will it work?" This coalesces into the next phase – Reality – which overshadows that initial glow of optimism.

One client, Helen, was working with me on her transition from corporate employee to business owner. Once she had quit, she still had to work out her three-month notice period.

In our session she was chomping at the bit to start her business, and getting more and more frustrated with her role and the politics. The toxic culture was starting to erode her confidence. So I asked her if it was possible to get 'gardening leave', where she could stay away from work but still be paid during her notice period. This would enable her to be able to work full-time on her business.

In our next session, Helen was jubilant as she had been approved the gardening leave. Three months on full pay and the freedom to start her business! All the energy that was being consumed by the thought of leaving the daily corporate grind was now released. She was feeling liberated and full of anticipation for her new life.

Phase 2: Reality

You miss the routine of getting up and dressed for the office. You have yet to establish a way to get out of your pajamas before noon. You long for the banter over the coffee machine about the latest TV show. Not having anyone to bounce ideas off makes you realise that you are all alone. You begin to feel sad and miss the people you have left behind.

Your to-do list appears infinite as there is much to complete to start up the business. In this phase, the initial novelty of having control over your time and how you spend it starts to wear thin. You miss the structure and routine of going into work, and you miss the infrastructure to get things done.

And suddenly, cold realisation sets in: For your business to succeed, it's completely up to you. Many decisions to make, precious money to invest and people to start calling.

Doubt creeps in as you wonder how you will possibly get everything done and start trading to make money.

Sylvana Caloni was Executive Vice President of Bankers Trust. After fifteen years the company was sold and her role was made redundant. Rather than continue to analyse and invest in other companies she decided to start her own consultancy, SC Executive Coaching, which upskills corporate leaders to make them more successful in their business environments. Despite her success, there have been moments where she's missed the big-business structure of her old workplace.

"I miss the comradeship of working in multiple teams and across departments, talking to other people who could act as sounding boards and bouncing ideas with them. I also miss the whole backup and the support system," says Sylvana. "I had to deal with the phone company today, whereas before I would devolve the problem to my staff. I don't have a marketing department doing the preparations for road shows and marketing materials. Previously you would just ask someone to do something, they would do it and it would be done. Now I have to do all of that myself. It requires me to be more creative and more disciplined in managing my time."

Phase 3: Shock

As the Reality stage sets in, so does more work, more isolation and more doubt. You may start to question if you can make it happen. The fear creeps in as you constantly stretch and operate outside of your comfort zone to do all that needs to be done. Sales don't happen as fast as you would like and the business plan looks like a fantasy. Even though you are working long hours and think obsessively about your business.

You are not sure about how to talk about what you do, and what your identity is anymore. You find it hard to "sell" yourself, your business, as it all seems too close to you. Your fear of rejection can stop you picking up the phone to entice prospects to work with you or buy your products. You can get stuck in the minutiae of setting up the business. Working in this detail saps your energy.

> You question yourself at every step – this is the grey zone of crossing over. You may even think, "Oh c**p what have I done?"

Maria Johnson knows this feeling well from her first few years as a business owner: "It's very difficult to go from working alongside other professionals which is fulfilling in terms of your mindset and sharing ideas. Going from a very high-paced environment, surrounded by super-intelligent people, to being home on my own was a shock. At first it was exciting and a bit scary but six months in you think 'this is not exactly what I thought it would be like. I'm on my own there's no one to ask for advice that I don't have to pay'. I felt isolated and I began to feel a bit scared; 'If this doesn't work out what have I done?'"

At this stage it is easy to feel like a victim, out of control and not sure what to do next.

Phase 4: Slump

If the Shock continues, you will start to enter the Slump.

> Low energy, low motivation and wondering, "Are all the long hours for less money really worth it?"

You may be fed up with the red tape, or maybe you are still searching for funding or that big customer.

Chapter 8: The transition to being a Corporate Crossover

You feel isolated as you are working hard by yourself to get the business moving. This is the time when another job starts to look like a good option. Should you get real and get a job? This stage represents the greatest risk of you returning to being an employee again.

This will probably happen to you as well – you will accept that this is the choice you have made. The acceptance moves you into the Adjustment phase.

It was during my slump phase in London that the foundation for Corporate Crossovers was born. I spent 18 months in a languid phase of inertia, looking for jobs and also running my executive coaching business. If I'm honest, I didn't do either particularly well at that time. I would do my best for my coaching clients, and then in the back of my mind be preparing for job interviews. Two things happened that made me get clear on my decision to stay self-employed:

1. I was sitting in an interview with a Big Four consulting firm, silently saying, "Don't give me the job," as I knew I would be back to high strategy and selling solutions I didn't really care about.

2. Adding up my invoices in my office, I realised I was making more money than in my last job. Wow – that really fired me up. At that moment, my two-year-old daughter came up to my office and told me lunch was ready. So I realised I could still do what I really loved, earn great money and spend time with my children. In that moment I was determined to grow my business. I accepted my choices and decided to move forward.

Phase 5: Adjustment

In this phase, optimism returns and your energy rises. The vision you have of your business being successful becomes tantalisingly real again. You start to get more wins, and you feel things are finally moving in the right direction.

You start to build your new identity. You find yourself talking less about what you used to do for a job, and more about the business you have created and your role in that.

You now know how to talk about what you do and you do so with pride. Those difficult start-up problems have been solved. You are feeling more confident about your income stream.

Your isolation has lessened because you have connected with other business owners like you, through networking groups and local associations. They understand what you are going through and can offer advice, support or company when you need to have a change of scene. New friendships are forming that start to replace those former office friendships.

Your days and weeks have more rhythm to them and that supports you. There is a structure to your time that works.

You and your business start to receive positive feedback and your confidence grows.

Galia Orme from CHOC Chick explains how she moved to this stage: "I really missed getting up, dressing up for work and having a laugh with work colleagues and going out for a drink afterwards. Within months of leaving my job, I joined a local "women in business" network. I think it is important to surround yourself with people who want you to do well and believe in you. Having people around you, having a business mentor, and having networking and support groups is essential."

Phase 6: Momentum

You have adjusted to your new life and are fully reconciled with your decision to leave your job. You accept that you no longer have the framework of your old employer and you have replaced that with your own creation, to fit around your wants and needs. Your feeling of isolation has subsided as you become an active networker, making connections and spotting opportunities.

Financially you have adjusted to the peaks and troughs of income flow and you are feeling confident that your sales pipeline is healthy. You have also found the right support, realising that you don't have to do it all or find all the answers by yourself. You have updated your criteria to judge whether or not you are successful, as you realise your old constructs of success don't hold true for you anymore.

> "It's those thrilling times, thrilling to the power of two, because you miss some of the padding, you miss the people who can help you, and you miss the corporate credit card. There is a ton of risk, but I am not afraid to be afraid, I'm not afraid to take risks," says Julie Anixter.

You can start to see a direct impact between your effort and the success of your business. This enhances your confidence and builds your momentum.

You start to talk about your business more enthusiastically; the vision you dreamed of becomes even closer to being attained.

Phase 7: Commitment

The business flows with grace and ease. You continue to get brilliant feedback and you are feeling much more positive about the future. Your knowledge of the business has grown and you understand more about how the business ticks; what levers you need to pull to reduce costs, increase sales and manage profitability. You feel a great deal of pride in your offering and can see the potential of it more clearly than ever before. Your identity and your business are closely meshed.

93

You can't ever imagine going back to your old life.

> "Right now, my mindset is pretty fearless," says Dee Poku. "It's weird when I think about that person who was terrified about asking! I really feel like I have evolved and my mindset is very 'can do'; everything feels possible if I want it to be. That's just a great place to be."

9 How to transition smoothly

Travelling through the transition

The journey through the Corporate Crossover Transition Model is a personal experience. You will go through this transition in a completely different way than anyone else. The time and depth of emotion in each phase will be different for everyone too. You may move back and forth between a phase or two. This is natural; be kind to yourself if this happens.

The transition can be made easier, shallower and less traumatic. There are both practical, external exercises and deeper, internal reflections that will smooth the transition. You may move through one transition, only then to go 'backwards' a few months later and revisit a previous phase. The transition is an individual journey. Even if you leave your job and set up at the same time as someone else, you will go through your transition at a different pace.

There are five factors that will influence how you move through the phases.

1. **How you leave your job**
   - What were the circumstances – did you leave, or were you pushed?
   - How was your confidence and self-esteem when you left?

2. **How much you 'are' your job**

   - Is your identity tied to your title and old organisation?

3. **How you judge success**

   - As you leave the corporate world, these criteria for success change. We need to update these as we leave

4. **Identity and money**

   - What does money represent for you? Are you the sole income provider?

5. **Support**

   - What support do you have as you cross over?

   - What is the size and quality of your network?

1. How you leave your job

For a smooth transition: Leave your job with a compelling vision, a well-thought-out business plan, eight months' savings and your confidence intact. If you did, this will help you flow through the Corporate Crossovers transition model much easier. You have the clarity, confidence and commitment to move through the phases smoothly.

What could slow you down? Sadly, we don't often experience an ideal world as outlined above. You may have been managed out, taking redundancy after surviving a tough trading environment where morale was low and you worried constantly about who would be next to leave. Or you may have quit, deciding that another insensitive comment, attack on your ability or lack of appreciation for your hard work and commitment was the straw that broke the camel's back.

Circumstances of leaving

The circumstances of your leaving will determine how you feel about starting your business. Were you pleased to go, shocked, resentful, or a mix? However you feel, acceptance is very important to help you move on and move forward.

How do you accept the reality of your departure? Spend as much time as you need reflecting on your leaving circumstances.

If it was painful, think about

- what you did like about your old job
- what you learnt
- the people you've met
- your achievements.

Now consider the benefits of no longer being there.

If you are running a story in your head about your leaving circumstances, and wishing you had said x or done y, then **stop the story**. Revisiting it time and time again will keep you stuck, you will create a deep neural network around it.

You will become addicted to your story of leaving and it will inhibit your forward progress.

Your level of confidence and self-esteem.

From my research of 300 Corporate Crossovers, I know that toxic culture is cited as the key reason women leave to set up their own businesses.

In some cases, this environment can damage your self-esteem and confidence. If your decisions have been continually overturned, or if you have been bullied, passed over for promotion, or neglected in salary reviews and bonuses, your confidence can diminish.

Owning your own business will require you to get out there, sell yourself, and do new things as you create your business. It will test your confidence every day.

If you left your job with your confidence well under 100%, starting a new business will be tough for you. You will question yourself and your decisions more each day. You will find yourself arriving at the "slump" phase sooner.

If your confidence is high, and self-esteem intact, then starting out on your journey as a Corporate Crossover will be much easier. Complete these exercises to grow your confidence and keep it high.

Exercise: Self-appraisal

You can download the worksheet to accompany this exercise at www.corporatecrossovers.com/when-its-time

It can be very easy to forget how much we have done, our past successes and our skills. A self-appraisal allows you to remember all that you have achieved in your life so far, both personally and professionally. When I do the following exercises with clients, they are always pleasantly surprised at how much they have achieved and the knowledge they have acquired.

Recalling these achievements is a wonderful way to boost your confidence!

1. Write down 10 successes you have had which are relevant to your new business (personal and professional).

2. Write down 10 skills and experiences you have what will enable you to make your new business a success.

Chapter 9: How to transition smoothly

This is much more than a review of your CV, it is a deeper reflection on your past experiences, both personal and professional.

> This self-appraisal will allow you to remember and reflect on what you have done in the past which will help you in the future.

Often we forget what we have done to get us where we are today, and I find that this reflection exercise is beneficial in affirming our progress to date. It is a wonderful reminder of all that we have achieved and thus a great way to nurture our confidence.

Exercise: Success Shower

You can download the worksheet to accompany this exercise at www.corporatecrossovers.com/when-its-time

We are all busy. And when we run our own business, we get even busier. So often we forget what we have achieved as our minds become focused on what else there is to do, or what we haven't done. As humans we are programmed to think about the issues and problems instead of the achievements and successes. This is a well-designed protection mechanism. By finishing each day and reflecting on what has gone well, we replenish our belief that we are achieving a lot, that we are making a difference and that things are going well.

Every day write down three things that you did well. At the end of every day, take 10 minutes to reflect on the day that has been. Ask yourself: "What have I achieved today?" and "What's gone well?"

> Buy a special journal and write down three things that you have achieved and have gone well every day.

Very quickly this notebook will be filled with your achievements. When you hit a rough patch and wonder "What have I done?", simply pick up your notebook and cast your eyes over your past achievements. This simple tool will boost you and give you the motivation to continue.

2. How much you 'are' your job

For a smooth transition: You evaluate your identity and update it so it aligns with your new role.

What could slow you down? You could find it hard to make the switch from the status and identity definition that your corporate role, title and salary used to give you.

What we call ourselves, how we explain what we do now all point to how we feel about our identity.

> When we leave our jobs to start up our own business, our identity changes.

When I think about my own transition, this was the most painful part of all. I was my job, my title. I didn't think of myself as a wife or mother, but first and foremost as a General Manager for a FTSE 100. Leaving this title behind – and my associated self-esteem and identity – was much harder than I could have ever imagined.

> When we have a job it can be easy to use the status and position that it gives us as our de facto identity. We relate more to our title and company name than to who we are without them.

I know from my own experience that I didn't really think that deeply about who I was and my real identity until I left my corporate job ten years ago. Stripped of my office, business card and impressive title, I was unsure how to introduce myself, and how I would talk about who I was. Feeling exposed without this bestowed status, I had to rebuild my identity and determine who I was and how I would describe myself and what I did.

> A Corporate Crossover comments: "I was surprised how leaving affected my sense of identity. Even though I didn't enjoy my old job, I had been doing it for many years and it had become part of my sense of who I am."

Stepping out and promoting ourselves and our own services instead of that of a well-known corporate brand name can be hard. It is even harder when over the years we have inextricably linked who we are and how we view ourselves with our title and employer.

> As a former solicitor for a top London law firm, Emma Arkell found this aspect of her crossover very difficult: "I struggled and still struggle with the loss of status and the loss of regard that you have when you are in that sort of job. Regard from everyone – fellow professionals and people generally – if you're a high flying solicitor doing top-of-the-range cases."

When asked "What do you do?" at a dinner party, you may have had a slight blush of pride as you recounted your title and company name, and your questioner may have had an impressed look on their face. Contrast that to answering the same question as a business owner. How do you feel? How do you articulate what you do and the name of your company? And how do you respond to that person's reaction – with a warm blush of pride? Or do you quickly add, "Well, I used to be a senior executive at Big Multinational Bank"?

> When she left her senior job at the bank, Sylvana Caloni missed the instant impact of her old title: "I miss not having the gravitas or the entry point that you have when you're a very senior executive. When I'd go to Japan with my analysts, the fact that I was an executive vice president of a multinational bank would guarantee that we would get access to corporate and government leaders. The fact that I'm a solopreneur can present challenges in terms of access. So I work harder to create alliances and networks than I used to do in order to overcome the challenges."

"Occupational identity"[2] is a sociological term that describes how your self-image and career are entwined. Occupational identity provides an avenue for validation by others and, of course, validation of yourself. This validation can boost your self-esteem and make you feel good about yourself, your work and the value you bring. Occupational identity also provides a fuller sense of "self" by providing a role or personality type with which to identify.

My transition from an employee for a well-known global company to searching unsuccessfully for a position in a foreign country deepened my identity crisis. I didn't know who I really was without my title and company brand.

Observing other Corporate Crossovers, I can gauge where they are in their transition curve by how they introduce themselves. Those early in the process still add a qualifier to their new position: "I'm Wendy, and my business is Corporate Crossovers, and I used to be a General Manager at FT.com." They still need the status and identity boost that their old position and company gives them.

[2] Kessler, R. C., Turner, J.B., & House, J. S. (1988). The effects of unemployment on health in a community survey: Main, modifying, and mediating effects. Journal of Social Issues, 44(4), 69-86.

Chapter 9: How to transition smoothly

As social psychologist Everett Hughes[3] said: "A man's work is one of the things by which he is judged, and certainly one of the more significant things by which he judges himself. Many people in our society work in named occupations. The names are tags, a combination of price tag and calling card. One has only to hear casual conversation to sense how important these tags are."

> The strength of our occupational identity will determine the ease with which we transition from our former role as an employee to our new role of business owner.

Shifting from a role that gave us pride and self-worth (even if we are frustrated and repelled by the toxic culture) into a new business start-up can be shaky. It can leave us questioning who we are, what we offer and what value we add.

Another Corporate Crossover says: "The realisation of how much personal credibility is tied to the name of your company was a revelation. Because I had only worked for Fortune 500s and had operated at a director level for a number of years, it was difficult to adjust to the loss of status that belonging to a well-respected company brings. Of course I had personal networks who recognised me for who I am and what I do. But for new meetings I have never had to explain who we are and what we do before."

Many of us have been bought up to believe that what we accomplish is directly correlated to our self-worth. Growing up, we were given praise if we achieved well at school or at sport. Our sense of self-worth grew as we were acknowledged. Even in those early years our identity

---

[3] Hughes, Everett C. "Men and their work"; Published by FreePress 1958

was being melded with what we did. And in our minds our worth often came from those accomplishments and the accompanying praise.

As adults, this relationship between accomplishment and self-worth still exists. It is another reason why when we leave the traditional confines of the workplace behind that we can feel adrift and uncertain at a very deep level.

"It was an identity crisis. After 20-plus years inside it was weird and strange now not to have that corporate identity and association. It took about a year to re-gear that aspect of my personal power and identity," says another Corporate Crossover.

Updating your identity

When you have welded your self-identity to that of your former employer, it can make the journey through the phases of the Corporate Crossover Transition Model harder.

Taking time to reflect on how you viewed yourself in your previous role is an essential step to beginning the process of updating your identity. Doing this means you are accepting of who you *were* and who you are *now*.

Identity evolves and we are always learning, adapting and growing. Our view of our identity gives us the framework by which we subconsciously operate. I like to think of it as our internal operating system, just like on a computer or smart phone. If we don't update our internal operating system, we can make decisions and behave in ways that are not relevant to who we are now.

In the busy-ness of our lives, we often neglect to update the core part of who we are.

Taking time to update your identity will establish your foundation to move forward.

Chapter 9: How to transition smoothly

Exercise: Update your identity

You can download the worksheet to accompany this exercise at
www.corporatecrossovers.com/when-its-time

Work through these steps below to update your identity or your
internal operating system.

1. Describe the sense of purpose your previous job gave you.

2. What meaning did it have for you?

3. How did you describe yourself in your old role? What adjectives
   and phrases did you use?

4. How did you feel when you described yourself?

5. What sense of purpose does your new business give you?

6. How do you describe yourself now? If you have yet to give
   yourself a title – make one up! Think beyond 'real' job titles
   and create something unique.

7. How do you feel about the description?

8. Do you feel differently about the two descriptions, your old job
   versus your new business? If so, what is the difference in your
   feelings?

9. What do you need to adjust to feel aligned with your new role?

Do take some time out and reflect on the answers. Chances are that
you have some deep neural pathways to climb out of as you update
your self-identity. Reflect on your updated identity every day. Ask:
What is my framework now? That will help you feel successful and
content with your new role and decision.

3. How do you judge success?

For a smooth transition: Redefine success to encompass your new priorities and your new company, and decide what's really important.

What could slow you down? Losing sight of the fact that the goalposts have moved. Trying to judge your new role by the measures you used to judge your previous role.

Success is a big word. It's a word we all know and use frequently yet it has as many different meanings and measures as there are people that use the word. It's a concept that we use to define ourselves and, if we are honest, others. Even with its frequency of use, it's a concept we rarely update when we consider how successful we are as our roles change and evolve over the years.

> Subconsciously we are always judging how successful we are. Whether it be self-imposed success criteria, or judging ourselves against others.

When you work as an employee, your success criteria are often based on those external markers given to you by your company: salary, title, benefits, staff and other perks. These can be your measures of success in the corporate world.

When you set up your own business you are changing many things: what you do, your title, your working structure and your place of work. But very rarely do you update your success criteria.

One of my clients, Sarah, had been a marketing manager for a leading retailer in the UK. Whilst she had crossed over and her new business was going well, she constantly derided her success. When I asked her what was underneath the non-acceptance of her success, Sarah realised that she was still working with her old success model. She had loved the prestige of representing a huge household brand and the large budgets she worked with.

At a deeper level, she realised she was still comparing herself with her university friends. These friends had gone on to work in the financial markets and were earning very high salaries. When we unpicked this a little more, she realised that whilst they were earning high salaries, they were sacrificing personal time and all were still searching for their ideal life partner. Sarah became more honest with herself and realised that her competitive nature and comparing herself to her university friends was stopping her from feeling successful.

Together we took the time to discover what was most important in her life and how her choices were enabling her to satisfy her priorities. She realised that the choices her friends made would not have allowed her to meet her deepest needs. Knowing that, she could accept her choices and move on.

> Leaving the world of work behind can be extremely exhilarating and it can also be massively challenging – sometimes on the same day, or even the same hour.

It can be easy in the transition phase to feel as if you are not a success any longer. But your new measures of success can be very different. This personal definition of success will be different for everyone. You will have one definition of success for you as an individual, and a separate one for your business. Of course the two are related but, as you would expect, they will have different elements to them.

Some of the factors that could be included in your new measures of success are:

- Freedom
- Leisure time
- Family time
- Autonomy
- Flexibility

- Business growth
- Income
- Gross turnover
- Brand recognition
- Diversity of clients

Maria Johnson, knows that as a successful management consultant she knew exactly how to measure her success – money and happy customers. "If you had a customer that kept giving you business you were more successful if the customer was satisfied. It would make the firm more profitable therefore you were remunerated well."

Since starting Eddie Catz, her view has changed. She still ranks happy customers as one of her measures of success, but now freedom and a sense of achievement have replaced money on the list of important criteria.

"Now success means the freedom to pick up and take a month and be with my family. I realise I am the master of my own destiny," says Maria. "We have a lot more flexibility to do what we want when we want. Hopefully when it stops being fun we'll be in a position to sell our business and do something else. At the moment for me success is my freedom and also the satisfaction of having built something. Probably one of the best compliments is when I hear a teenager saying; "You own Eddie Catz? Wow I grew up in that place. I loved it."

Working with many Corporate Crossovers, I know they can often feel as if they are failing in their venture when in fact their business is operating well. So I ask them, "When did you last redefine your criteria for success?

Most of the time, they haven't taken the time to really ponder and define what success means for them now. What happens when the constructs that we defined our success (and sometimes ourselves) by are no longer there? Does this mean we aren't successful?

> Starting up your own business means redefining many things: finances, working location and tax status. But while you set up all these new systems, your model for success may be stuck at your old workplace.

Not redefining your success criteria can leave you with that nagging doubt, wondering if you made the right decision to leave. If left unchecked, it can also grow into vacillation about whether to stay self-employed or to go and get a 'real' job again.

I went through an eighteen-month period of wondering if I should 'get real' and get a job, and it wasn't until I took stock and thought about what success meant to me now in my own business that I realised how successful I was.

Taking stock for me involved:

- Examining what was REALLY important to me about the life I wanted to live (my values)
- How much time I spent working now versus before (daily hours and vacation)
- My income
- Comparing my stress levels with now and before
- Focusing on myself and not comparing myself with former peers

After my period of reflection all those years ago – I was stunned! Stunned at how much money I was earning with low stress and lots more time for my own pursuits. That was the real turning point for me to grab hold of my business with both hands and fully commit! That was the moment the temptation to go back to a corporate job vanished completely and permanently.

I also realised that I had a different criteria for my personal success than my business success.

My idea of personal success now includes:

- Living my values
- The difference I make to people
- What legacy I leave behind
- Having freedom and flexibility
- Having autonomy

Success for my business includes:

- Building a well-known brand
- Having an impact on customers
- Meeting my financial targets

Many of the Corporate Crossovers I spoke to for this book have had similar experiences about their own success criteria changing so much.

So whether you have recently left corporate to start up your own venture, or you have been doing it for some years, take some time to reflect deeply on what your success criteria are now.

Dee Poku's success in her roles at the various movie studios was strongly tied to the company's brand itself. Success for her meant working at a well-known company, "A nice title, I was paid okay, not great but okay. The perks that came with working for a company like that help you feel successful. You work on award-winning movies, go to premieres, travel to glamorous places, but these were all kind of peripheral. When I think about it, I wasn't always paid what I was worth, but everything else kept me there. It was just the perception; the way I was perceived made me feel successful."

Years later, running a successful marketing consultancy, Dee has a different view of success:

"Once you start your own business, your achievements are all your own and that's an amazing thing. When you've pitched a client or conducted a successful campaign for somebody. It was all you, through your efforts, obviously with support, but ultimately the buck stops with you and it was yours. The autonomy was incredible, just the choice to decide who you wanted to work with, in what capacity, the who and the how and why was completely yours and that's very empowering. As opposed to having to sit in a meeting, potentially having your ideas rejected, having to go with a plan of action that you might not agree with, that your boss wants, this was different. This was all you. The autonomy in particular made me feel successful. Whether you were right or wrong, you'd made the decision."

Exercise: Update your success criteria!

You can download the worksheet to accompany this exercise at www.corporatecrossovers.com/when-its-time

Step 1: Acknowledge the Past

When you had a job, how did you define your success?

Write down ten elements that were important to you and made you think you were succeeding.

(Some ideas to help you along: impact on the bottom line, working with a large team on important projects, doing something that made a tangible difference to people, salary, business class travel, meeting with senior decision makers, large budgets, feeling respected, working for a great brand, job title...)

Step 2: What's precious now?

What is most precious to you now? How do you want to spend your time and your energy? What are your dearest values?

Write down between five and ten areas that are really key to you now.

(Some ideas to help you along... Independence, feeling like I make a difference, family, variety, freedom, financial security, time with children, state of mind, time to pursue other interests beyond work, working with people I like, creativity, opportunity, growth...)

Step 3: Take a measure

Reflect on your 'Precious Now' list. How much is your current work and personal life reflecting those values? Are you successful when measured against your new standards?

How does it compare to your past criteria of success? What do you think when you compare the two lists?

As we go through our life we are constantly evolving. Our values may shift and evolve to represent who we are in that moment.

It's important we feel successful on our terms as when we *feel* successful and *believe* in our success, more success comes our way.

4. Identity and money

Your relationship with money is a significant factor in what your journey through the transition will be like. It's not only the amount of money to cover your living expenses, but also what that money represents to you in terms of status, identity and success.

> The change in financial circumstances is a significant transition for a Corporate Crossover.

The regular payments into your bank account from your employer – irrespective of how you are feeling about your job or how productive you have been – provide an economic cushion and a certain level of status. These disappear as you embark on starting up your own business. Suddenly, income can be both lower and more erratic than what you have previously enjoyed.

And it's not only the salary. It's also the related benefits, healthcare, company car, expense account and so forth.

Money and crossing over relates both to status and financial security. Having a regular income allows us to spend confidently knowing that our bank account will be replenished. We can buy those things we want to make us feel good. In some cases we are buying things to make us feel better because we are so unhappy in our jobs.

As a Corporate Crossover commented when asked how they adjusted to earning less money, "Sometimes I miss the buying power that I used to have. But it came at a price. I have a better lifestyle now with less money. I used to spend much of my earnings on making myself feel better."

That little moment of pleasure derived from the purchase and that belief that "I deserve this because I've been working so hard in such a toxic environment," or "I need this to cheer me up after such a stressful week at work."

Your salary, benefits and other perks of your role (the international travel, five-star hotels and expense account dining) all add to your feeling of status. You can feel proud and privileged in your identity because of these external measures of success. When they vanish you can feel as if your status has declined.

> "It is difficult and I do miss the days when I used to get paid double what I am making, but I was a lot more materialistic then also," one Corporate Crossover reflects. "I have learned that I do not need all the latest clothes! I do miss my two holidays a year, but I know that will come again, once my business is thriving. I am investing in my future and one where I can be myself and truly happy."

The impact of the regular income ceasing is significant. Should the business revenue be uncertain or slow to gain momentum, this can add enormous stress to a start-up business owner. Especially if she is the sole breadwinner.

Exercise: My relationship with money

You can download the worksheet to accompany this exercise at www.corporatecrossovers.com/when-its-time

Consider what your current level of salary means to you. Take some time to examine this deeply. Ask yourself these questions and write down the answers:

1. If you earn a 'good' income, by what criteria do you judge it to be 'good'?

2. Why is that important to you?

3. If you feel pride in the amount you are earning, what in your new venture that will also give you that sense of pride?

4. Do you judge people by how much you perceive them to be earning? Ask yourself, why is income level a criterion you judge people by?

5. How will you really feel about yourself if it takes your business one or two years to allow you to reach your current income level?

6. Considering the way in which you spend your disposable income, how much of it is to make yourself feel good? Are there other ways to still get this same feeling?

Sometimes money is less of an issue of how much we earn, but how we make it, and what we have left behind.

Vicki, a coaching client, left a well-paid job in corporate to follow her passion, retraining as a make-up artist, with a vision of creating a successful consultancy and a line of premium skincare products.

A regular income was important to her but it was even more important to her parents. In our coaching sessions she told me how her parents worried about her and her income. They questioned her about why she left a successful career to start all over again. Vicki knew in her heart that she was much happier but she was unable to convince her parents.

We worked together and she realised she needed to revisit her decisions to remind herself why starting her own business was a great idea. Once she convinced herself and checked in again with her big reason why, she was able to speak about her decision more confidently with her parents. This confidence blossomed into how she spoke to prospects and converted into more business.

And while around 70% of Corporate Crossovers don't make the same money they earned in the corporate sector, for many that's a non-issue compared to the other benefits: "I can go back and earn $100,000-plus per year but I would be working day and night, travelling every week and seeing my health suffer," one woman told me. "Yes, I now hardly make any money but my health has improved, my home life is great and I have more time with my husband."

5. Support

For a smooth transition: Build your network before you leave your job, join groups that will allow you to talk to other people in similar circumstances, and look after the family members and friends who stand by you.

What could slow you down? Not having a built-in network when you leave your job, having to build a network from scratch and having nobody to talk to who understands what you're going through.

"Have I done the right thing? Have I made the best decision? Am I good enough? Do I really have the skills and experience to make this work?"

This never-ending self-questioning can deplete your confidence and erode your business success. You can start to feel paralysed by self-doubt. You don't take the bold actions required to move the business forward. Until you leave your job and start your business, you can't know this.

> Having your own business is a huge catalyst for introspection and increased self-awareness.

As business owners, your internal mechanisms are intrinsically linked with the external performance of our business – simply put, if your head and heart aren't in it, the business won't succeed.

Chapter 9: How to transition smoothly

This meshing of your internal and external worlds can come as a surprise. After a long successful career in the corporate sector, you may take for granted your success and your ability to do your role well. You know that on the whole, you have what it takes to do the job. If you question things, it is more likely to be the ability of others and the culture you are working within rather than your own ability and performance. Suddenly, in charge of your own business, you realise that the buck now stops with you. You are what lies between where you are now and the future success of your business. This can be overwhelming for some, invigorating for others.

There is no one else to blame. Taking responsibility for your business also means taking responsibility for yourself and your actions. This is where your mind can impede you or propel you. Finding the right support for your state of mind is essential for the success of your company.

The most common sources of this moral and emotional support are partners, family and friends. Leaving the corporate world means losing that framework, so you need people around you to help prop you up.

> You need to have someone who will support you, who sees your potential and that of your business.

If you're stuck in a job you hate, it can be impossible to imagine you could ever miss going into the office, but many of the women I interviewed said exactly that.

"I didn't think I'd ever say it – I miss going into the office! I miss the relationships. It can get lonely working from home."

Forty-two per cent of the respondents in the Corporate Crossovers survey felt this way. Social banter, colleagues to bounce ideas off and to socialise with – this was the highest-ranked item on the list of what they missed the most. They missed the social connections even more than they missed the consistent income.

If left unchecked, the loneliness can be debilitating, and sap your confidence. As one woman explains: "I am a people person and did not realise why I was becoming depressed working in my home office alone."

At a deep level we all need to be accepted as part of a group and feel a sense of social belonging. This need for social recognition can be linked to our basic need of feeling valued and appreciated by others. Maslow in his Hierarchy of Needs[4] identified this as a need for 'belongingness and love'. This can be satisfied through relationships with family, friends and (of course) work colleagues.

MASLOW HIERARCHY OF NEEDS

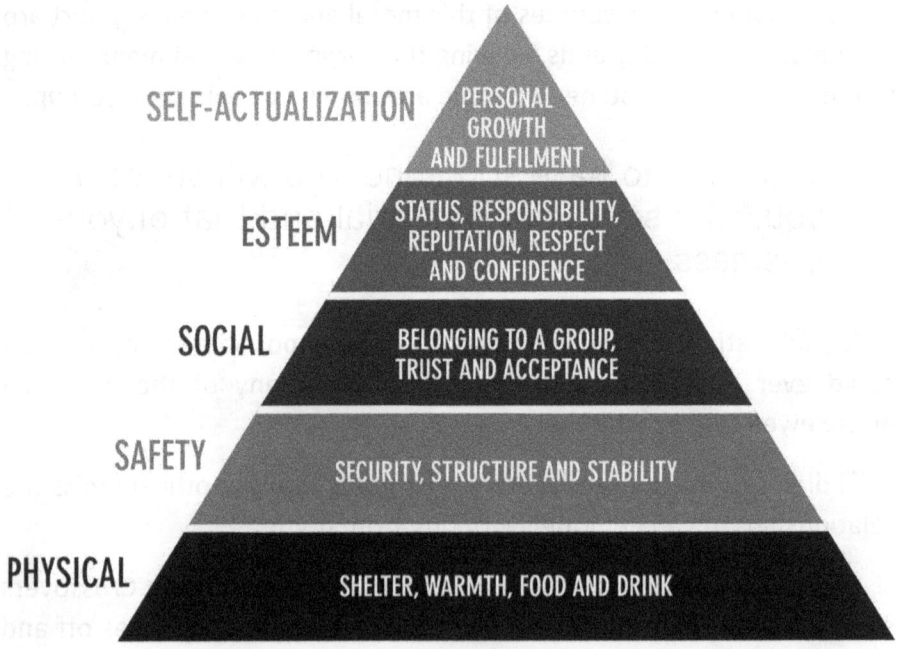

SELF-ACTUALIZATION — PERSONAL GROWTH AND FULFILMENT

ESTEEM — STATUS, RESPONSIBILITY, REPUTATION, RESPECT AND CONFIDENCE

SOCIAL — BELONGING TO A GROUP, TRUST AND ACCEPTANCE

SAFETY — SECURITY, STRUCTURE AND STABILITY

PHYSICAL — SHELTER, WARMTH, FOOD AND DRINK

[4] Maslow, A. H. (1943). A Theory of Human Motivation. Psychological Review, 50, 370-96.

Chapter 9: How to transition smoothly

For five days a week you've been surrounded by work colleagues. If you leave that and start going to work alone, you have lost a huge part of your 'belongingness and love'. If we continue up Maslow's Hierarchy, the next level is Esteem. If you are lacking in 'belongingness and love', you will not be able to maintain your self-esteem. In fact you will feel low, and lacking in confidence to make the calls you must to build the business. You will question your status and your esteem may start to crumble.

Returning to London from Tokyo and launching my Executive Coaching business, I felt very isolated. I had left my friends and new-found professional network in Tokyo, and I had yet to recreate those connections in my new home. I remember longing to belong... anywhere. I would often walk into clients' offices and yearn to be part of a meeting I saw taking place, no matter what they were talking about!

As the months progressed, I eventually found a new set of connections, rekindled old relationships and I started to feel like I belonged here. That made me happier. It gave me more confidence and I felt more committed to my path of remaining a business owner. Had I not felt this belonging and instead remained in isolation, I am in no doubt I would have returned to the corporate world. Even with my past experiences of toxic culture, poor leadership and extreme politics.

If you are feeling isolated, it can make doing that one bold thing to grow your business really tough. There is no-one to spur you on, no-one to acknowledge your success and how hard you tried. That companionship, the feeling that we are all in it together, even if it is crap, motivates us and gives us a sense of buoyancy.

Crossing over from corporate to your own business, you need that support. You need to feel that you are not in this alone and that there are other like-minded people out there.

While you may not have someone to directly discuss the latest TV show with, you will have someone who understands what it is like to leave that environment behind and set up on your own.

Sylvana Caloni came to London from Australia before she started up her Executive Coaching business. She says: "I've come to realise the importance of networks. When I came to London I didn't have relationships in London, I knew one ex-broker and one ex-colleague. That was about it. I didn't have networks here, so it wasn't easy. It helped me recognize just how critical networks are: endorsers, champions, people opening doors or making suggestions or challenging … that sort of thing."

Everyone I spoke to for this book reinforced the critical importance of having a large and strong network. And if you can build it while you are still employed, even better.

When I moved to Tokyo, I knew no-one. I had to befriend strangers in a very big city. But thanks to the internet and a few networking groups, I started to reach out and ask those people who seemed interesting to me to meet for a coffee. Just to talk. I discovered that most people will meet you for a coffee once. And they will be very gracious about it. What happens after that will depend on your chemistry, potential synergy and opportunities in keeping the relationship alive. Eventually I had a large network, and that is where my clients came from. I had built up visibility, a relationship and, most importantly, trust. Once this was established, then the business opportunities began to arrive.

The network you build up while you are working can be a potential source of clients for you when you start up.

Trisha Proud of Partners In Solutions knows what a difference her network made to her business: "The relationships I'd built up whilst

> working meant that if I wanted information about anything I could reach out to people and they would be responsive. I didn't have to hunt down the business."

As you develop and grow your network, you never know how you will need it. So nurture it, give back to it regularly with no expectation and remember business karma.

Building good relationships now and maintaining them is a great investment for the future.

Laura Bergerson left the corporate world 14 years ago, but the positive benefits of the network she built there are still helping her companies today.

"I think the network that I built while I was in the corporate world has really sealed my client base today. Many of those people are no longer with those companies and they've gone on to other companies. When I started, I called everyone I knew in the channel and said, 'Hey I'm available, this is what I'm doing. I would love to provide these services to you.' They were like, 'Great, this is terrific, we had no idea you were available.' I started getting so much work I didn't know what to do with it. I think that those past relationships made it easier for me to bring on new business."

Building a network is an easy undertaking, whether you are working or not. If you are still working, don't make the mistake I did of being insular and complacent. Use every opportunity to meet new and different people. Industry conferences, launch events, suppliers, agencies, even people you travel up and down in the elevator with that don't work in your office but work in your building. If you can't reach out and even say hello to them and start a chat because this is too far out of your comfort zone, then maybe running your own business isn't for you.

And once you make a network, maintaining your network is simple. Dropping people a quick email with an article you think they may be interested in, making an introduction that you think will benefit them, helping them when they ask. The key to maintaining a vibrant network is to be giving more than you take. You need to add value to the relationships, give support, make relevant introductions and send helpful information.

10 Replacing the office framework

Creating a new working routine

No more commuting, no more pointless long meetings, no politics, and the freedom to do whatever you choose with your time. Bliss!

Leaving employment feels like freedom. You become your own boss, you choose who you work with, you choose how to spend your time. Isn't this why you left the constraints of the corporate world?

The freedom and control you have over your time when you leave your job is fantastic. You relish the chance to spend your days how you want, escaping the deadlines and the planning cycles of your old job, as well as the demands of your old boss and clients.

> Without the daily routine that working in an organisation provides, your desired freedom can seem like an ocean of possibilities.

The downside is that you can start to feel as though you are drowning with no structure upon which to float and navigate to your destination. You get tossed and turned by whatever is happening during the day, as opposed to steering your own course single-mindedly.

You may feel that you have all the time in the world; that you can easily do those household chores or meet a friend for a quick coffee.

But if you let these non-business building tasks eat away into your time, you will still be in start-up mode a year later. It is critical to treat your time as if it was cash. Do you invest your time as wisely as you invest your money into the business?

Structuring your time when you leave the corporate environment is essential to starting off well.

You need to think and act exactly as if you have a normal full-time job. This can be hard to do. It can be particularly hard on women, especially when you work from home and double as the key manager of the household. The attraction of quickly putting a load of washing on becomes more important than calling a sales prospect. In reality, this is a delaying tactic to stop you getting down to the work and stretching your comfort zone to start generating business and income. Essential as clean clothes are, they will not add any revenue to your business.

It feels liberating and uplifting having a lovely tidy house, until you realise that your business isn't performing as well as you had hoped. And then you take a look at your bank balance, and with a sharp intake of breath you see that your savings to fund your business have been whittled down.

> "Since I started working from home, my house has never been cleaner, my family more well-fed or my internet shopping bill so high. And I bought a lot of stationery," admits Claire, who left a senior job in a government agency to run her own consultancy business from home. "Why didn't I do my work first? The chores were easier than doing my work and if I could see a pile of washing out of the corner of my eye it completely distracted me from working. I didn't do the work, and when deadlines approached, I had to run around like a crazy woman."

Chapter 10: Replacing the office framework

> Claire soon realised that she was going to need some discipline in order for her business to succeed. She had her upstairs attic space converted into an office, so she could work without being distracted by household tasks. Not everyone will want to go to those lengths, but it was the perfect solution for Claire, who can step into her office and truly focus on her business.

To succeed when you crossover, you need to treat your time as if you were working for someone else.

Consider treating your business venture like a job.

Treat your business venture like a job

- Imagine if you started and finished working at the same time every day.

- Imagine if you got dressed for work even if you are sitting at the kitchen table.

- Imagine if you had a 'get started' routine that made you feel like you had started work that day.

- Imagine if you worked during your working day and weren't distracted by household chores.

Time is finite. When a day is finished, we never get it back. Time is one of the most precious resources of your business. To help your transition, recreate that rhythm of working that helped you to succeed as an employee.

> One of my clients, Tess, left a stressful 70-hour-a-week job in finance to start a wellbeing business. She came to see me after she had been out of her finance job for six months. In the first few

months, she admitted to me that she "played" at her business. When I asked her about this, she realised that when she left her job, she was physically and emotionally depleted.

In hindsight, Tess realised she should have taken some time off to have a real holiday. This would have enabled her to rejuvenate and recharge, so she would have had more energy for her business start-up. We worked together to create a structure to her week that gave her boundaries between her work and personal time. Creating time not only for work, but also for much needed relaxing so that she could replenish her energy.

Once she understood this, Tess was able to start thinking of her new time as if she was working; this helped her feel more productive. This physical time structure helped to change her mindset.

Working for yourself: How to transition

1. A Start-the-day routine

What did your start-the-day routine look like in your old job? For me, as I got off the bus, I would stop and pick up a coffee to enjoy at my desk. Sitting down in my office, sipping my coffee and planning my day got me into the rhythm of work. I felt like my day had started.

Can you use your routine to help you ease
into your new job?

When I moved to Tokyo and found it hard to get revved up after dropping my son at nursery, I did this again. I found a take-out coffee shop, ordered my favourite and zoomed home. Sitting at my desk, I planned my day sipping my coffee and, strangely, felt like I was working again.

Chapter 10: Replacing the office framework

Think about your start-the-day routine:

- Did you read the newspaper on your way into work to feel on top of current affairs?

- Would you walk to work to get your exercise in for the day and arrive with a clear head?

- Did you go to a coffee shop en route to the office to plan your day and get ready for meetings?

- Did you read the same three news sites online for fifteen minutes before starting work?

What can you do to give yourself that 'starting work' mindset every day?

Among my home-based clients, many find it essential to leave the house before they start their working day. Whether it's taking the dog for a walk, dropping the kids at school or getting a coffee, leaving the house means they are dressed and interacting with the outside world before they return home.

Hannah is a client who has an expanding accounting and bookkeeping business. She had spent a lot of time helping her clients get their businesses under control but she was frustrated that she never had time to get her own company in control. When we discussed her daily routine, she told me that she got up, turned her computer on, and before she knew it, it was lunch time; she had lost half the day- often on unplanned tasks – before she even realised what time it was.

To help her feel in control and to give her breathing space at the start of the day, she decided that the first thing she would do was to have coffee at her local coffee shop every morning.

Taking time to get out of the house, think about her business and plan her day helped her feel in control of her business again. She got her thinking time back, and she could start to create systems for her own business.

---

2. Structure the week

In one of my early coaching sessions – as a client – I complained to my coach that my diary was jam-packed. It was like it had exploded and taken on a life of its own. She then asked me a very simple question, "Well, Wendy, who actually puts those appointments in your diary?"

Well, duh, it was me. I then had a fabulous light bulb moment and realised that I needed to take control of my diary. This meant me putting myself first and structuring my week. When I worked for my last employer, my weekly structure was dictated by the re-occurrence of weekly meetings, planning cycles, one to ones with my direct reports and so on. Working by myself, I had none of that.

> After that lightbulb moment I realised I was sabotaging my effectiveness with my overwhelming schedule.

In the past I used to run about all over the city to lots of meetings and networking events five days a week. Often it would take me an hour to commute in, and an hour to get back. This meant I was spending a lot of time travelling back and forth to meetings, wasting precious time I couldn't use to work. My travel time would sometimes be as much as ten hours a week. My output was decreasing and I didn't have time to really think. I certainly had no time to work 'on' my business. I decided to get tough with my diary and only do certain things on certain days.

I restructured my week and now it looks like this:

Monday: Work from Office
Spend time planning my week, have my mastermind call, my marketing call and write articles.

Tuesday: Work from Office
Create courses, create the marketing campaign, and (if it's the

last Tuesday of the month) spend time reviewing my longer range plans.

Wednesday: Work from office or meet clients

Thursday: This is the day I run workshops face to face or virtually. Do more client work.

Friday: Out and about networking and meeting new people. I do this on a Friday as everyone's diary seems to be much easier to get into. It took time to get used to being so disciplined but now I do it, I love it. It works for me because I have more time and I feel in control.

Having practised this way of structuring my week for so long now, means that it is easy for me to say no to people when they want to meet me on a day that isn't a pre-designated meeting day. The time I have gained by using this structure is worth the effort.

3. Plan your day into time boxes

This is much more than just writing a to-do list. This is really about planning to use your time effectively to build your business.

> Structuring your day into chunks to do certain types of activities is very efficient.

Plan your day as follows:

1. **Must do first**

   What are the things that MUST get done today to move your business forward? Refer back to your business goals. What must be done today to move towards achieving them? Schedule time to do these FIRST. Even before you open your email, before you return those calls. If you don't spend time working on those things that will grow your business, it will stagnate.

It is too easy to get pulled into tasks that seem urgent, over and above the important work to build your business.

2. **Be mercenary with email**

    Plan two time slots for email. Do not have your email open all day. I doubt you need to be that immediately available. I do mine in the late morning and then last thing in the afternoon. It is switched off at all other times. By doing this *I* control my day, not the people sending me emails.

3. **Collate your calls**

    If you have to make a lot of calls, group them together and do them one after the other. This will get you into the rhythm and free time up later for other things.

4. **Time to create**

    Writing, planning, those tasks that need you to think... Always schedule a block of three hours of completely uninterrupted time. The only way you will get the work done is if you actually make the time for it and focus on it. Remove other distractions and enjoy having the space to work.

5. **Be selective with social media**

    Manage this like email. Choose two or three times a day when you will check and update. Set a limit on your time. I have clients that use a timer set for fifteen minutes. This helps them to be more efficient when they go into the social media world.

With more planning and forethought you can effectively create more time.

4. Get outside assistance

It isn't healthy to work non-stop. When you have your own business you can be consumed by all the tasks you need to complete. You need

Chapter 10: Replacing the office framework

to stop and smell the roses, to meet people. You need to have new experiences to stimulate your thinking and to gain a fresh perspective. The wonderful thing about being in charge of your time is that you can make this happen.

If you have friends badgering you to meet up for coffee, attend a class or you want to do some volunteering, do it. Just schedule it in.

Use these outside structures to help you add more structure to your week. By scheduling these non-work activities in, you won't feel guilty about doing them, as you know you will have allocated the time you need to do your work around this.

Nikki, a client who ran an HR consulting business, changed her business model so she could consult more independently instead of being based in her clients' offices. This meant she could work from home. Living in Tokyo, she had a small one bedroom apartment. When we started to work together, she felt her work was taking over her life. There was no physical separation between her personal life and her work life. Her work files, her books and tools were interspersed with her novels, personal mementos and her leisure space.

Realising that her physical environment was contributing to her feeling of being overwhelmed, Nicki reorganised the space in her apartment. One end of the living room was designated for her workspace. She bought a funky room divider, behind which she placed her desk and work files. She then reorganised her bookshelves and had a separation between her work and leisure reading. Having the screen enabled her to close away her work at the end of the day, giving her a visual and physical break.

Does your working environment support your business?

Where are you working from? Have you hired a beautiful serviced office with a wonderful view and natural light, or are you perched at the end of the dining room table? Or maybe it is something in between. Have you found a corner in the spare room, which also serves as the junk room and then the guest suite when visitors roll in?

Consider whether or not the space you are in is serving you and your business in the best way possible. Do you feel like you are in a place to work and create revenue, or does this feel like an afterthought? The acid test is, would you have a client visit your work space? If yes, great! If not review what you are doing and where you are doing it. It may be that you never invite clients or customers to your space, but it is a mindset.

Factors to consider when you are reviewing your working environment:

1. Physical space

Do you have enough room to spread your material out, with resources to hand so you don't waste precious time always searching for them? Do you have dedicated shelf or storage space so you can keep your area tidy and well-organised?

It is important to make your working space inviting and appealing so you feel compelled to spend time there.

2. The vibe

This may sound a little strange, but does it 'feel' like a place to work? When you sit down to work, are you able to focus or are there distractions? When we stretch our comfort zone to build our business, we will procrastinate. If you are working in a space that has distractions, it will be harder for you to focus when you need to.

3. Noise

If you have to make phone calls, do you need privacy or a very quiet environment? It may be that you like having a buzz around you, so you feel less isolated. It is important that you feel comfortable – with as little or as much privacy as you need – in order to make you feel comfortable and productive.

Being your own boss! How do you stay accountable?

You are running a business. You have no manager, no task master or externally set objectives to drive you. It is all up to you. Suddenly, being completely accountable and having to motivate yourself to drive the business forward to reach your goals is entirely your responsibility.

- Does it matter if you don't make this month's targets?
- Will you get fired for not turning up to work three days in a row?
- And so what if the customer's order is five weeks late in the delivery?
- Who will reprimand your behaviour or attitude?

A significant transition in crossing over is having to self-manage.

One Corporate Crossover comments: "Time management was the one thing I really had to concentrate on to make this business work. When I worked for someone else, I knew when to arrive, when to leave, how much time should be spent on a particular task, etc. Working for myself, I have to be cognisant of how much of my time is allocated to each client's work."

The fields of opportunity can quickly disappear if you don't become your own manager. You must be smart about how your precious resources of time, energy and money are being used to best effect. And you must keep yourself accountable to deadlines, targets and goals. If you don't, the time will slip by and you will feel like you have been very busy when in fact the business has not moved forward at all.

1. Take time to review the business, and to work 'on' it.

Making time to review our plans and progress against them is key. Many of my clients will schedule time in their diaries to review their business plan and then something more important comes up. That meeting with themselves to work 'on' the business never happens.

Of course, working with a coach or business mentor does give you that time to review and work on your business, but that support may not be appropriate to you.

> I discussed this issue in a review with Imogen, who ran a virtual assistance business. She found that one of the most valuable results of the coaching was the time to work 'on' her business, and to plan her future activities. She decided to use our regular weekly coaching slot as her time to review her business.
>
> To ensure this happened in the future, beyond the coaching, Imogen not only put it in her diary but she arranged for a fellow business associate to meet her in a cafe, where they would both review their businesses by themselves before catching up over coffee.
>
> By being accountable to meeting up with someone else, that important review time did not get replaced by other tasks.

2. Creating a plan

Imogen has a plan to review against. From my experience with coaching and workshop clients, many of them don't have a plan. As cheesy as this sounds, my first marketing director drummed into my very impressionable brain: "If you fail to plan, you plan to fail".

The thought of creating a business plan can turn the most passionate entrepreneur pale. Many of us think a business plan should be created as an exhaustive programme of scenarios, numbers and scary accounting formulae and jargon. You believe that once a plan is done, you can throw it into your bottom draw.

No. You must have a plan. Before you take the leap from the regular, reliable income, your familiar occupational identity and the framework of the office environment, create a plan for your business.

The best business plans are living, breathing documents. They represent your heart's desire. They show you where your customers will come from, how you will attract them and how the money will flow, in and out of the business.

They will allow you to consider the products or services you are offering to your market, at what price. And what will make you different to the competition.

A plan forces you to detail your business dream onto paper. The discipline of writing the plan will give more energy to your ideas and the structure to give you the confidence to move forward. It will help you see what assistance you will need and when, what resources you need to use and what knowledge you need to acquire. Getting your ideas out of your mind will also help you create new ideas. By getting your thinking out of your head, you can feel as if you have more space and more opportunity to grow.

And when you have a plan, you have something to measure your progress against.

> Recently, I worked with Michelle, who had left her job in an architecture firm to set up her own practice. She had a great portfolio, a big black book of contacts and a fabulous website showcasing her talents. Yet, she felt she was working much harder than in her last job, and not making anywhere near the same money.
>
> When I asked her how she was performing against her plan, she looked blank. She didn't have a plan. And when I asked after her goals, she told me that she just wanted to make more than she used to in her last role.
>
> Michelle is very typical of many of the business owners I meet. No goal, and no plan to achieve them.
>
> We set about creating a compelling set of goals for Michelle to reach and a simple plan to help her achieve them. The goals were simple to set; she just asked herself these questions:
>
> - How much do I want to invoice this year?
> - How many clients will I need to reach my invoice target?
>
> The first part of the plan was being very clear about who her ideal client would be. Then she could identify how she could reach them and focus her efforts around that. We brainstormed some ideas for client acquisition and then set about laying them out in a plan.
>
> In our next session, Michelle was much more upbeat, as she felt confident that the work she was doing was effective against her goals and plans. She was able to check her progress against the plan we had made previously. She could see how her work was impacting her results.

Chapter 10: Replacing the office framework

Reviewing your progress against the business plan can be a fantastic opportunity to reflect on what you have done, how far you have come and what you have achieved. Use it as a great way to mark your journey in the world of a Corporate Crossover!

11 Growing your business

There are two important aspects of business growth:

1. Growth from the inside out – your mindset.
2. Structural growth – your business and financial frameworks.

Whilst these may seem to be at opposite ends of the thinking spectrum – one more esoteric, the other logical – they are, without doubt, interrelated.

Having excellent frameworks and structures in place gives you confidence that you are in control of the business operations and that you have a business that is scalable. Your thinking and your self-belief give you the motivation to invest time, money and energy into your business to create those structures. Neither can exist without the other.

Grow your business from the inside out

How do you introduce yourself? It might seem like a minor question, but it raises a major issue. When I attended a high-calibre event in London during International Women's Day, I was able to listen to speakers with incredible success stories, from Members of Parliament to multi-millionaire business owners. The audience of businesswomen and entrepreneurs were bursting with questions for the inspiring speakers.

As each woman got up to ask her question, she would introduce herself and say, "I'm Sally Smith and I have a very small business

Chapter 11: Growing your business

which..." Without exception, they all used adjectives such as 'little', 'small', and 'tiny' to describe their businesses. By using that very word they instantly belittled their own business. If you, as the business owner, can't speak proudly and confidently about your business, then who will? And what value do you place on yourself and the business?

> Your business is a reflection of your mindset. How you think about your business is ultimately what it will become.

You've left your job, you have a business idea that you are crazy passionate about and you even have your eight months' savings stashed away. But what is it really like running your own business? Is it really the entrepreneurial dream? Do customers come flocking to you as soon as you open your doors? Do you have the time to create the life of your dreams?

Sadly not. During the course of my research I was consistently told: "I never realised how hard it would be to start my own business and then make it work". Having your own business and making it a success will call on your deepest resources of resilience, commitment to the idea, energy and tenacity.

Sally Preston, founder of Babylicious, admits, "At times I wanted to stop... It was very tough. But my passion and the want to make a step change in my life kept me going."

When you are running your own business, you take the success or failure of the business much more personally than you would as an employee. When something goes wrong in your job, you get over it. It may cause frustration and stress but, at the end of the day, you most likely still have your job and your income. When it is your own business, mistakes linger longer, you internalise them more and they feel much more personal.

139

> Running your business becomes much more like an intense personal development experience.

As your business grows, *you* grow. And to grow your business, you need to stretch yourself past previously discovered limits. You need to break past your comfort zone.

Everyone I speak to who has crossed over talks about how much they have learnt about themselves. When you run your own company you are tested every day, your confidence will be pushed to its limits, your courage tried and your comfort zone stretched. Think about this in a positive way when it happens to you, because it means that you are growing and your business will too.

Managing brain chat

When you have your own business, you think you have all the power. And you do... mostly. But there's one thing in your life that you might find is more powerful than you would like it to be. In fact, it can be so powerful it stops you from succeeding. It is that little voice in your head – your brain chat. You give this chat so much power that you believe what it says, whether or not it is speaking the truth.

Like it or not, that brain chat determines your results. Your mindset will determine your outcomes. If you find that surprising, you're going to love this next point: You can control your brain chat!

> You can control what you are thinking, how often you think it and whether or not you believe it.

This can be a revelation for many people. You can control your thinking, and by thinking something else, you will get a different result. This means taking total responsibility for your thoughts, your actions and your outcomes. Of course you can't choose what happens in your life and your business but you *can* choose how you respond to it.

It all comes down to perception; essentially, your brain chat.

Imagine you are standing in the queue for the Post Office at lunchtime needing to post an application that must go today by special delivery. Already waiting 30 minutes, you are looking at the people in front of you who are all holding very large parcels for posting. You have an external deadline for a proposal at 5pm that day and you know you need all the time you can get to complete that task on time.

You can probably imagine how your brain chat might sound: "How slow is this queue? Why did everyone have to choose today to post their massive parcels? And why did they all have to come in at lunch time? I'll never get back to the office in time; I'll be late for that deadline. I'll never get that proposal finished properly; I won't win the business. Damn – this day has been bad and I just know it's only going to get worse."

Finally, you get to the counter, you are gruff to the assistant and he is just as gruff back to you. Then you drive back to your office in a bad mood and everyone seems to be cutting you off. You are so wound up, you find it hard to settle at your desk and do the work for the deadline. You just make it but feel really annoyed that you didn't have more time to do a great job. But you're not surprised, the day started off bad and just got worse. You can only hope tomorrow will be better. You've let your Post Office brain chat ruin your whole day.

Imagine if your brain chat had been like this: "How slow is this queue? I guess everyone else has decided to post their parcels at lunch time, too. Mmm, at this rate I may be a bit late getting back to the office. I wonder what I can do to help me get ready for that deadline whilst I'm in the line? Oh, I'll call that guy for the quote he promised, and then I'll know what I need to charge. Or maybe I'll just think about the key points of my proposal and that will save me time later."

You get to the counter, you feel relatively relaxed and have a nice interaction with the Post Office assistant. You then drive calmly back to the office, knowing that you made the best of the time in the queue, rather than getting wound up over something entirely beyond your control. You sit at your desk feeling grateful that at least you had some time to make that phone call and think about the points you need to make in the document. You send off the document in time, and feel happy that it's done.

BRAIN CHAT IMPACT

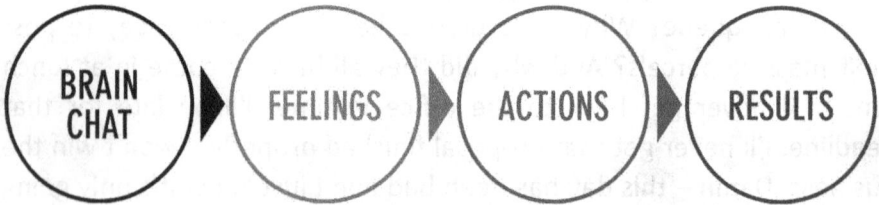

Same situation, different brain chat, different outcome.

> Mindset is a critical factor in your business and, of course, your life.

Impact of brain chat

"Whether we think we can or we think we can't, we're right," said Henry Ford, and this totally holds true with your mindset and your business. When you leave your corporate job and go to set up on your own, your brain chat can go into overdrive. You will give yourself excuses about why things can't be done, about why you are not good enough, why you don't deserve success, why everything you do is doomed to failure, and on it goes.

Chapter 11: Growing your business

As you start to get into action to make your goals a reality, do you sometimes hear a little voice in your head judging, questioning or even doubting your ability to follow through and gain the success you planned?

Imagine if your friend said, "You should give up this business idea, you can't run a business, go back and get a real job!" or, "You can't charge that! What gives you the audacity to think you are worth that much?" Chances are you wouldn't remain friends for long.

> Yet we put up with this shabby behaviour from ourselves all the time.

I had a very bad case of this self-sabotage recently when I launched my new Corporate Crossovers email newsletter. My brain was hectoring me with a wide range of unsupportive and critical thoughts as I went to sleep the night before the big launch. "You are crazy to launch a new business!" and "You should just stay doing what you are doing – it's so easy," and "You should go back and get a job."

And then I recognised my destructive pattern from a few years ago when I left corporate to set up my own business – yes, the words were slightly different but the big idea was the same: "Don't change," and "Keep playing small."

I felt grateful that I had caught it – yet, surprised that I still had it. I'm a coach, helping people with their own brain chat, but I was letting my own brain chat off its leash.

You know what? They are all just thoughts. They are extremely powerful as they will determine your reality if you choose to believe them. So, if you believe you're having a bad day, you'll put off making that important call. If you tell yourself, "I'm no good at sales," you'll never try hard enough. How can you judge your sales ability if you don't even try it out?

Built in protection system

So why did this voice come and haunt me that night? And why does it come into my mind as I stretch out to reach my goals? The easy answer is that your brain is trying to protect you as you stretch and change. Your subconscious mind kicks into overdrive and sends you these unhelpful thoughts, which it hopes will protect you from harming yourself.

Subconsciously, we avoid change; our brain is programmed to keep us safe. This phenomenon is called 'homeostasis'. The primitive limbic part of our brain is always trying to prevent us from getting eaten by some unknown predator or killed by an unforeseen disaster. In these modern times, of course, there are no predators and the physical disasters are relatively few, yet our brain still strives to protect us.

How does this play out in the twenty-first century and in your business? Maybe this sounds familiar: You are about to undertake an activity that rationally you know will grow your business but you procrastinate and somehow you start to run out of time. Or the voice in your head convinces you that this is a ridiculous idea and that you really shouldn't do it. This is your brain protecting you from unforeseen disaster. You are being kept nice and safe in your current thinking zone.

This would be fine if you were living in a cave. But you are in the process of creating a business. A business you feel passionate about that needs to grow and be successful.

You need to overcome your resistance, stretch yourself and shift the limits of your thinking. Otherwise your business stays the same and growth evades you.

The good news is that you can override your subconscious and choose new thoughts that will help you to get what you want.

Chapter 11: Growing your business

How does this work? The brain is an amazing connection machine taking in all new information millisecond by millisecond since we were born. It then connects the new information in the short term memory with what is already there in the long term memory. It does this to save energy (by clearing it from our thinking brain) and to allow relatively easy retrieval of new information by connecting it to a strong neural pathway.

Neural pathways are essentially thoughts. They are formed by the little electrical impulses we have when we think. When we think the same thought over and over again that neural pathway gets stronger and deeper. Thus it becomes the easiest piece in your brain to connect with.

I like to think of new neural pathways (new thoughts, new beliefs, a new goal) like a little, tiny country lane just being formed in the grass as you walk on it for the first time. Deeper, stronger neural pathways (thoughts you may keep repeating to yourself over and over again – yes, like the brain trash tirade) are more like the M1 – a large eight-lane concrete motorway, linking together two vital areas, the north and south of England. It's much easier to drive down a motorway than to cut a new path through the country, and when the going gets tough your brain will tend to head back to the main road.

When we are attempting something new (getting ready for a sales meeting, about to send a new newsletter, launch a new product) our thinking about the event will be naturally drawn to the biggest neural pathway. If you have a habit of beating yourself up or a repetitive thought that you know holds you back, this is the thinking that will win through. It wins because it is the strongest, deepest thought you have about that subject. And in most cases we let this happen quite unconsciously.

The good news is that we can change this. We can control our brain chat and start to have an 'inner supporter' instead.

Imagine that! Imagine having your little voice say things like "You are great at sales," "People will love your new product," or "You have been successful before, you can do it this time." What a difference that would make!

The thing with brain chat, is that you can control it. When an unsupportive thought comes into your brain, observe it. Then actively choose another thought that will support you and your goals. So, if you think, "I'm no good at sales," observe it, then stop it and say instead, "I'm new at sales and I'm getting better every day." Or another example might be, "That person is far too busy to take my call." Choose instead, "That person may be busy, and I'll call anyway – we can always make a new time to speak."

The difference in the thought may seem subtle but the impact is huge. The unsupportive thought will paralyse you and you will do nothing. The supportive thought will move you into action and make it easier to get to where you want to go.

The way to do this is to make those little neural pathways that are like a freshly-trodden path through the grass into strong pathways like a motorway. Every time you repeat your positive thoughts you put down another layer of strengthening on your new pathway. Take control of your brain chat and use it to help you grow your business and become a success.

One of my clients, Juliet, believed that everyone and everything was against her. She never got the sale, everyone was too busy to see her and she wasn't getting paid what she was worth. She was blaming everyone for her situation. She also expected her situation to get worse.

Essentially, Juliet's brain chat sounded like this: "The world is against me. Nothing goes right. It's all too hard." She had the brain chat of a victim.

Gently making this observation, I asked her – What could you think differently to get a different view of the world?

At first Juliet stumbled. Her victim brain chat was as firmly engrained as the M1. Then, with me insisting that she could control her thinking, she considered a different range of thoughts. She thought, "I could go and meet my client for coffee and ask him why he chose my competitor". "I could do more networking to find different clients." "I could accept where I am now and move forward." These thoughts helped her to get into action with a fresh viewpoint.

Importantly, Juliet realised that if she wanted to change her situation, she had to change her mindset.

Exercise: Taking control of your brain chat

You can download the worksheet to accompany this exercise at www.corporatecrossovers.com/when-its-time

When you are besieged by brain chat, and you want to move forward, try this simple process:

1. Choose a supportive thought
2. Write it down
3. Put it somewhere visible
4. Repeat, repeat, repeat!

The key with this is to repeat these thoughts frequently. You want to create a very strong and deep neural pathway so this new, supportive thought is the one that pops into your mind unconsciously.

One more thing you need to do is to observe your thinking.

You can control your thinking and the first step to doing this is to actually notice what you think. Slow down, be mindful and observe what you think.

Then when you do notice your inner critic speaking, replace that thought with your new supportive thought. This will take practice until it feels natural and easy to do. Persevere – it will make all the difference when you start stretching out to reach your goals.

Stretching ourselves

As adults we know that pain eventually goes away. So why do we resist the perceived pain that stretching ourselves past self-imposed limits will bring? To create and grow a business, we have to do things that we haven't done before, and demonstrate more tenacity and resilience than ever before.

Why are we fearful of putting ourselves out there, of making those phone calls we know will grow our business, when there is no physical pain involved?

Sometimes the biggest crossover transition of all is that you have to show yourself to the world. There is no corporate brand to hide behind or to use as a platform. You have to promote and sell yourself. And that can feel scary. There is no corporate framework to support you. Your learning curve is very steep. All decisions are yours. On the one hand this is liberating; on the other hand it can be paralysing. You can feel overwhelmed – and then stuck – by the number of decisions you need to make.

Your own business becomes a representation of who you are.

Deciding to crossover is a monumental decision representing change and, for many of us, a fearful time as we jump into the abyss. Yet, we all survive. What no-one tells you is that that is just the beginning of facing your fears and continually stretching past your known limits.

As you start creating your new business, you have to learn how to work differently. You stretch yourself to learn new skills to complete tasks. To continue the growth even when the business is established, it is essential to expand your approach. This sounds very easy and logical on paper yet when you try to do it, you can meet with resistance.

Your comfortable ways of thinking and doing are being stretched and you may find this unenjoyable or even unpleasant. Remember, it is your brain just trying to keep you safe by avoiding change. We can control our thinking... and still stay safe!

> Each time you step out of your comfort zone
> in one area, your whole comfort zone expands.

The bigger your comfort zone, the more you will feel comfortable doing. Over time, those things that may scare you now or that you have resistance to won't seem like that anymore – they will be just a part of what you do every day.

I worked with a client named Rachel who wanted to change her business model from being service-based to product-based. Rather than selling her time, she wanted to start selling courses. And she realised that a key part of her strategy was to do more public speaking and to raise her profile.

But Rachel hated speaking in public. She knew she would have to get over that fear to succeed in her new vision for her business.

So together we created a series of small steps for her to take. Rachel began with speaking opportunities with small audiences that allowed her to increase her confidence. By the time her launch date came about she was so well-practiced at smaller events that a

---

> big one seemed a logical step rather than a terrifying ordeal.
>
> By doing it in small increments, her comfort zone was stretched gradually and the whole experience was less scary for her.

Stretching yourself can be done in small increments... The key thing is to do it! Using external commitments as a way to make yourself stretch and grow is a very effective strategy.

So, when you feel resistance to stretching yourself, how do you move through it and get closer to your vision? From working with hundreds of clients over the years, I have found the following exercises to be very helpful.

Connect deeply with your vision

You may know in your head where you want your business to be in five years, but have you created a tangible artefact of this?

- Have you written down your goals, your ideas?
- Have you created a vision for your business?

A business vision is a statement that represents a future of what we want to achieve. It encompasses our dreams, hopes and aspirations. It is simultaneously concrete and abstract, and it holds both vivid and realistic possibilities. It is a wonderful combination of our big hairy audacious goal, and the emotional impact of achieving that.

Getting your ideas and goals out of your head and onto paper in a tangible form that you can see and touch every day brings the vision of your future closer and makes it more real. This starts to make the gap smaller between the future vision and where you are right now.

The easiest way to create a vision for your business is to start with a vision board. This is a collage of images, words, photos, etc. that represent your desires for your business in five years' time.

Chapter 11: Growing your business

Whilst the idea of a vision board may seem a bit 'woo-woo', they *do* work in changing the wiring in your brain. Once your vision board is complete, and you begin to look at it every day, the neural pathways about your aspirations for the business will be strengthened. The repeated viewing will focus your thinking on what you want, and make you more attuned to taking the right actions to bring your vision board to life.

Let's not forget the emotions! When you look at your vision board, you will most likely feel happier, excited and inspired. These wonderful emotions will produce the feel good neuropeptides in your brain – oxytocin and dopamine. With this positive cocktail running through your nervous system, you will feel energised and motivated to take action.

I love vision boards! They are inspiring and motivating and most of all they are great fun to make!

Exercise: How to create your vision board

You can download the worksheet to accompany this exercise at www.corporatecrossovers.com/when-its-time

Set aside a few hours when you won't be disturbed. Settle yourself into a place where you feel comfortable and can spread out. Take a range of your favourite magazines and a pair of scissors. Also find a big piece of paper or card, and some glue.

Step 1: Creating

Taking a few deep breaths, concentrate and be mindful. Imagine what your business will be like in five years, what you want to achieve, how you want your business to be. As you are leafing through the magazine, consider these questions:

- Who would be your favourite customers?
- What types of activities are you doing?

- Where are you going about your business?
- What do you love about your life?
- Who are you learning from?
- Why are you doing this work?

Then pull out any images, photos, words or headlines that feel right about where you would like your business to be in five years. Next, arrange them onto a large piece of paper. It is an art – not a science – so don't question what you come up with, just do what feels right.

Step 2: What does it mean?

Now you have completed your vision board – it is time to interpret what the images mean to you.

Look at your vision board and ask yourself these questions:

- What will you be selling to your customers?
- What will they like about your business?
- Will you employ others, who will they be, what will they be like?
- What will your business look like (shop window, website, office, etc.)?
- What will your daily routine be like?
- How will this change your life?
- What will the business feel like?

To connect deeply with your vision for your business, look at your wonderful creation and the answers to your questions every day. Ponder what it means and feel the excitement that you experienced when you first created the board.

Remember: Each time you look at your vision board and reflect, you are creating new neural pathways. This neural network will help you to see more opportunities to help you achieve your vision.

Chapter 11: Growing your business

Exercise: Facing your fear

⬇ You can download the worksheet to accompany this exercise at www.corporatecrossovers.com/when-its-time

Often there is one clear reason that you play small and fail to live up to your true potential: fear. You make decisions and take action based on your fears, not your true values.

Try facing up to your fears. You can do this by journaling. Take some quiet time and write down what are your deepest, darkest fears about this course of action and achieving your vision. What keeps you playing small? Then ask: What are the worst things that could happen? What could you do if that were to happen?

This will lift the weight from your sub-conscious because when you know what the worst thing that could possibly happen is, it makes the fear manageable and containable. It removes the power. You will start to feel "So what if that happened?" You know you could do something to overcome it.

Annie, a client of mine, wanted to cease trading with her business partner. She had wanted to move on for about a year, as the business was not her main focus any longer. She wanted to place all of her energies into her new enterprise.

When I asked Annie when she was going to make the call to end the business partnership, she always promised to do it before our next session. When it didn't happen the second time, I asked her how she was feeling about making the call. "Scared," she said.

Scared of her partner reacting badly, yelling at her and going off the deep end. She didn't want the conflict. When I asked Annie what proof she had that Rachael (her business partner) might act this way, she had none. She realised it was all in her mind, built up over

> months of procrastination and worry. And sure enough, when she did make the call, her partner was amiable and agreed that separating was the right thing to do.
>
> There was a high cost to Annie's powerful imagination and fear – a year of procrastination and inability to focus solely on her new business.

Many of the successful crossovers I spoke to had been inspired by this quote from Eleanor Roosevelt: "You gain strength, courage and confidence by every experience in which you really stop to look fear in the face. You are able to say to yourself, 'I have lived through this horror. I can take the next thing that comes along.' You must do the thing you think you cannot do."

Often the thought of doing the act constrains us and holds us back. Then we realise, once we do it, there was nothing to be scared of.

Exercise: Reduce resistance by going bite size

You can download the worksheet to accompany this exercise at www.corporatecrossovers.com/when-its-time

We most often feel resistance when we think what we are going after is too big or even impossible. Sometimes our five-year vision or even our one-year goal can seem more like climbing Mt Everest as opposed to a nice stroll through the park.

The easiest way to make a goal seem attainable is to break it down into small components. So imagine your goal was a cake – what are the six ingredients you need for a cake? In what order do you add them to the bowl? What goes in first, and what happens right at the end?

Chapter 11: Growing your business

Think about your business like this… if your goal is to make 100,000 and you are currently making 50,000, what are the key activities you must do to double your revenue?

Maybe the smaller steps could be something as follows:

Step 1: Analyse what 50,000 represents (the number of customers, products sold, etc.)

Step 2: Analyse where you can find your biggest customers

Step 3: Raise your profile and promote yourself

Step 4: Consider whether you can raise the revenue of your current customers

Step 5: Ask current clients what type of new products they would like, and create those products

Step 6: Advertise new products to your existing customers as well as your potential ones found in Step 2

Step 7: Repeat

Of course, depending on your goal, the steps will be different. But the key thing is to break down the big goal into smaller chunks. Then the stretch you have to take from your comfort zone is smaller (and, therefore, more comfortable) than doing it all in one go.

The great thing about making your goals into bite-size pieces is that it allows you to focus on what is in front of you.

Removing the worry about what you can't control gives you the energy to focus and feel more in control of what you are doing.

Angela, from her vision board of wanting to earn good money in her interior design business, broke her annual financial target into the number of clients that represented at her average fee. She then broke that into how many clients she needed to work with each month. From this she was able to frame her marketing plan, by understanding how many potential clients she had to attract into her sales funnel and then convert.

Be kind to yourself; make the stretch to playing big enjoyable! Success is the combination of all the small things you do every day.

Growing your business structure

I've often wondered why some businesses erupt and are huge, enabling the owner to have financial freedom, whilst others, with an equally valid value proposition stay small, providing just an income and if we're honest, another job.

What is your real reason for starting up your own business? Is it to design the lifestyle you want, or is it to create a profitable business complete with exit strategy?

And are the two necessarily exclusive? I don't think they are. Yet this is a major stumbling block for many women business owners. From research I conducted of 300 women who are Corporate Crossovers, 68% of them are earning less now than when they had a job. They may have a business which offers them the potential to create a large and profitable business but, for various reasons, they are not exploiting it in that way.

To create a business which is scalable, and that will provide financial freedom instead of just an income, you need to think quite differently about your business from the start.

When you are creating it, you need to build it with the thought that you will not be doing it all. Develop systems and processes from the start, so that you can automate as much as possible and ultimately have someone else to do this work.

You need to remove yourself from as much of the business as possible. Already I can hear those of you that are coaches, designers and other professional service providers saying, "But people buy *me*." You are thinking, "They want to buy me and *my* experience, *my* talent and *my* approach." That may be the case now, but you need to leave your ego behind if you truly want to create a big business.

Yes, they may want to buy you, but there is only one of you. If you continue to sell only you and your time, your business will be forever limited by how many hours you can work in a day.

Set up your business to scale easily:

1. Make the business about the *offering*, not you

Train your customers to love the approach of your business, your systems, but not to love you. In that way you can have them buy into the brand of your company and the company approach and philosophy, freeing yourself up from having to be pivotal to all delivery. Even if you are in professional services, you can adopt this approach and scale.

2. Systemise your approach

If you have certain ways of doing things that your customers love and it produces results for them, how can you create a system that you could train others in? These people that are trained up could become associates, employers, franchisees, or whatever. They would be able to service the demand you create for your offering in the same way you do. You get to cover a larger number of clients, even though you are not doing all the work.

3. Think big and think scale

Too often we are timid when we set our goals for our new business. Typically, women leaving corporate to set up their own businesses aren't wanting to create a huge corporation, as often the reason they create their own business is for more flexibility and freedom. Thus creating what they see as a big enterprise will not enable their lifestyle choice, so they are happy to get by and make enough to cover their costs.

From my experience many of them don't even have a business plan, they just start to work in their business, never giving time to think about 'what ifs' or 'how big could this be?"

Thinking about creating a larger business from the start, being diligent in creating a business plan and financial forecasts for growth, and ensuring you have the investment to underpin the growth, are essential to creating a business which will allow you to be financially free.

4. Exit strategy

Set up the business with a view to selling it one day. Imagine if you set your business up with this in mind. How would that influence your initial decisions about your business?

- What would you call your company?
- How would you package the services and products?
- How would you service your customers?
- What types of systems would you put in place at the start?

If you want to sell your business, plan your exit strategy at the start. At these initial planning stages you can be considerate of those factors you need for a sale.

Chapter 11: Growing your business

We deserve to have thriving businesses and to enjoy the benefits that brings, both financial and emotional, doing work we love and find rewarding.

12 Don't cancel the cleaner

Crossing over and starting your own business can be a journey of twists and turns.

At times you will feel exhilarated, excited and eagerly anticipating each day as it presents you with new opportunities and experiences. You will relish the freedom and flexibility of being your own boss. You will love doing the work that matches your values and is meaningful to you.

Sadly, it is not always like this. At other times you may feel as if you are taking two steps forward and three steps back. The business will test your resolve, your resilience and your self-belief. You may feel lonely, and as if no-one really understands what you are going through. You may also feel stuck with no-one to turn to, especially if they questioned your decision to leave your corporate job. Wanting to avoid the "I told you so," you resist reaching out for help, and risk feeling worse about your situation.

Starting out, as new Corporate Crossovers, many of the women I interviewed had little support. Often they felt too proud to ask or simply didn't know where to look. Others were just too busy to get help, preferring to do it all themselves and push through their issues. Long hours and sheer hard work were how they grew their enterprises.

Even though they may have done it themselves, in hindsight some of them wished they had found support earlier.

They now realise that having that extra support earlier could have made a significant difference to the speed and quality of success they experienced.

The support required differs for all Corporate Crossovers as it depends on their own skills, experience, personality and specific business issues being faced.

Risking a demotion!

It can be a shock when you set up and then run your business to find out just how much there is to do. The work can seem never-ending. Then, on top of the volume of tasks, chances are you have to tackle things that you have never done before.

Many women start up entirely by themselves and thus feel like they have to do it all themselves.

Curiously, many women then do it all. After years of managing departments and having personal assistants, when they start up on their own, they become their own assistant, secretary, travel organiser and cleaner.

The risks of trying to do it all include:

- Missing out on opportunities for doing the kind of work you really want to do

- Thinking you're saving money with your DIY approach, but costing yourself more high-paying work

- Feeling as though you have been demoted into the most menial job you've ever had – and you gave yourself the demotion

- Taking away your enjoyment and pride in your business
- Reducing your self-confidence
- Causing you to undervalue your time and expertise

You can't do everything!

There is so much to consider when you're starting up a business. Ranging from which legal entity is most appropriate, insurance, location, funding, banking, company name, marketing materials and on and on. The list can appear endless.

> Don't neglect to think about the support you need to make the money you used to earn.

As one recent Corporate Crossover commented: "I really wanted to get started with doing my coaching, but I find myself spending my time researching the legalities of setting up a business, designing my website, and deciding how I should do my marketing."

In the corporate world there's a framework where all of these things are handled, as if by magic, by another department in a different part of your building. You never think twice about what's needed to make a business run.

Suddenly, you are faced with it all. Chances are that you have not been trained in running all the aspects of a business. I ran large departments and start-ups within big corporates but I was still not prepared for the level of detail, breadth of work or the amount I needed to know and absorb very quickly. Welcome to a steep learning curve!

When you leave the corporate job, you don't know what you don't know. In a way, ignorance can be bliss when you first start out. But then the realities of having a business can hit home. Mistakes you make through lack of knowledge and experience can not only damage your business but also your confidence.

> One Corporate Crossover recalls her early days: "I have no regrets about taking the plunge to become an entrepreneur but I would have loved balanced, positive advice so that I could have laid a solid foundation straight away. The two camps offering advice seemed to be 1) Government schemes – all doom, gloom and negativity, and 2) Personal/business development seminars – a lot of rah, rah, rah and promoting getting rich quick. If I had had a steady six month programme or mentor perhaps I wouldn't have made some of the mistakes I made. The biggest challenge was the knock to my confidence, and that took quite a bit of working on before I was ready to risk growing the business again."

Don't be a DIY burnout

It seems that most Corporate Crossovers learn what they need to know on the job. Too busy to take courses, cash flow too tight to afford business coaching or a mentor, they knuckle down and do it themselves.

> There are times where this 'DIY' attitude can be an impediment. Doing things yourself to save money can actually end up costing your business money.

Because you are learning as you go, you may miss opportunities and hamper business growth. You can spend your time learning skills which could be outsourced to a lower cost resource. For example, website updating, book-keeping, diary management, etc.

You may also make some colossal mistakes which may take time to unravel. Certainly, not having the right business support, combined with the isolation, can make the transition to being a successful Corporate Crossover harder than it needs to be. Without timely and appropriate support, Corporate Crossovers can get stuck in The Shock or The Slump phases of the transition.

The feeling of the continual grind of tasks and work that you left behind in a more junior role some years ago, can leave you feeling demoralised and as if you have taken a backward step. This can keep you stuck in "slump" and not harnessing your energy productively to work on the big areas that will move your business forward.

> "I didn't come from a business background," says Emma Arkell. "I was a divorce lawyer so I have no business knowledge or retail knowledge. I've never had any experience either in business or retail so I was stepping out into the dark."

In other cases, the business model can be very simple and not require a lot of advice or complicated structures.

> As Zoe Sinclair recalls: "I had no business experience so I was really using common sense and nothing more than that. I was fortunate in that my idea meant that I didn't have to go to the banks for a loan. I didn't have to do anything complicated. It was get a client and start earning money; it was as simple as that."

It's not only the knowledge they lack but also how much work there is to do in creating, and then running their business that can be surprising.

Often business owners will treat their time as if it is free. In fact your time is not free, it is one of the most precious resources of any business.

Chapter 12: Don't cancel the cleaner

Just because you think you aren't paying for your time, you attribute no value to it. This misguided thinking leads to long hours and hard work. Business owners with this view realise that instead of creating a business to liberate them and give them the flexibility they desire, they have created another demanding and exhausting job and often for less pay.

Feeling overwhelmed by the variety and volume of tasks to be tackled when running a business can stall success. Often a woman will feel as if she is barely coping now with the workload, so if she was any more successful then she would be even busier. And who would want that? This simple assessment can lead women to subconsciously put the brakes on their growth as they just don't know how they would cope with more business.

Avoiding this trap is essential if you want to have a successful business and feel as if you are thriving. You want to feel as if you are loving what you do, feel in control and know that you can easily grow as your business becomes more successful.

A step change in how someone runs their business is when they start to value their time and leverage it better for growth.

> "Some of my biggest challenges came around running a very busy business and being very reliant upon people," says Chey Garland, who built up her outsourcing call centres into a business employing 3,100 people. "I assumed that everybody could do what I could do. And that they would have my passion and commitment. I think when I look back at myself as a very young entrepreneur, my expectation of people was too much really. I think that understanding how to work with people and how to bring the best out of them, and have give and take was a lesson I had to learn. Ultimately, it became very natural and really did bring out the best in my people."

Building your team

Accept that you are not an expert in everything. Accept that bringing on staff or outsourcing specific work to someone who is an expert will save you time, money and frustration. The person you employ or outsource to may take an hour to do the job it may have taken you six hours to do. Often tasks we need to do to keep the business functioning and legal can sap our energy and motivation. If there are tasks like this for you (mine is book-keeping) then outsource it and use that time on activities for business growth.

> Karen Silk, who now employs 26 staff, recalls how she started taking on employees in her first year of trading: "When I was totally on my own I was probably doing 12-hour days and weekends. I employed someone to do all the administration so I could just get rid of all that donkey work. If I hadn't had her I don't know if I would have made it. I would have probably ended up exhausted. The next person I took on was in finance. They did contracts, invoicing, debt collecting, agreeing contracts and all that which then just left me free to do the selling. I kept the selling to myself because I knew that's what I could do and I was good at it."

Many business owners fear taking on employees. They may be concerned that the business revenue isn't large or consistent enough to support paid employees, or that they do not want to deal with the perceived red-tape involved in employing staff.

Consider creating a team for your business that is virtual and outsourced.

This means that you can have the right skills and experience in your business without the financial and legal commitment of employing permanent staff. The cost of this support has decreased significantly over the years. With the growth of the virtual assistant industry and job bidding sites, it is now much easier than ever to get low-cost, just-in-time support in bite-size chunks. Having this level of flexibility for staff resourcing is beneficial, especially in the early stages where you are still establishing sales pipelines.

Getting the right support at the right time will enable you to focus on those activities where you add real value to enable your business to grow.

Spend your time like it was money

When you are employed you get paid day in and day out. You get paid if you have had a super-productive day or even if you have been staring wistfully out the window or doing online shopping. You don't need to worry about how much your time costs the company; you are more concerned with what you take home every month.

This experience can give you the impression that your time is free.

If we haven't had a job where we needed to bill our time to clients, we can be ignorant of what our time is worth. Whilst we are still working for someone else, that's all OK. It's when we leave and we decide to create our own business that we need to wake up and start placing a value on our time.

Many business owners think when they are completing a task, that it is costing their business nothing. They think because they are doing it, it is free.

> Every minute of your time has a cost associated with it.

That cost is the opportunity cost of what else you could be doing with that time instead of what you are doing now. Spending time on menial and non-revenue-producing tasks does not save your business money, it *costs* your business money because you could outsource those jobs to a lower cost resource and then spend that time doing something that produced more value for your business instead.

Just because you *can* do something doesn't mean you should. It can be easy to get addicted to doing a lot of small things which you think are moving the business forward whereas, in fact, they just keep it ticking over.

> To grow your business, you need to understand where the investment of your time will have the greatest leverage; where that investment will have the highest return.

A while ago I was completely weighed down with ten new coaching clients all starting at the same time, and all needing feedback reports created and written. Usually I do these myself, but I found another coach who was willing to do all of the 360-degree interviews (80 of them), and I outsourced the typing of the notes to my virtual assistant in India. All I had to do was edit the typing to create a great 360-degree feedback report for each of my clients. I still got paid for my normal work, but outsourced the heavy lifting where I knew I couldn't add value. It was cheaper for me to pay someone else to do the typing and interviewing so I could do higher-earning activities.

At this point in my business, I started to change how I valued my time. I saw where my real value was, what I was charging a premium for and also where I could outsource work. I was able to use the time that freed up for me to do business building activities to get more clients.

> If you viewed your time as if it was money, you would be much more cautious about how you spent it.

Chapter 12: Don't cancel the cleaner

If you spend an hour standing in the line at the Post Office, how much does that cost your business? How much value have you added to the business in that time? I would guess zero. Imagine if you had an assistant, who charged less than you, and they spent an hour in that line. Imagine what you could do with that extra time – call prospects, write a marketing email, create a new product idea… Wouldn't that be a better way to add true value to your business than spending your precious time in a queue? It's time to get real about what you are worth to your business and value your time differently.

You need to believe that you are worth it, and that you don't have to do all of the tasks involved in running your business. If you do this, you will never be able to scale and grow your business to the size that will support you.

Get professional help when you need it

Many of the women I spoke to got to bursting point before they sought help.

> There seems to be a belief system running among many business owners that "If I can do something, I will," as opposed to outsourcing the task or calling in experts.

This misguided belief can result in them spending time on tasks for the business which do not add value and can hamper growth. They are spending their precious time on tasks that could be easily outsourced to a lower cost resource.

After talking to 300 Corporate Crossovers, I discovered that the amount of work involved in setting up a business came as a big shock to nearly all of them. Many of the women did all the work themselves instead of outsourcing it. This caused them to lose sight of their business vision and forget what value it is that they bring to the business.

Often when business owners are spending a lot of time doing the more menial and repetitive tasks involved in setting up and maintaining a business, they can forget why they set it up in the first place. If you are not spending time doing what you love and adding value to your business, you will become demotivated and start to question if it's all worth it.

> To grow the business, *you*, the owner, must spend time adding *real* value, working 'on' it and crafting the business and marketing strategy to drive growth and gain new customers.

Step up and ask for support when you need it.

People will help when asked. They love to help. Think of it as 'business karma'. What goes around comes around. Most of the longer-term business owners I interviewed had asked for help and advice early on and it had been offered willingly. Now they want to give back and help as well. One day you will be in that position of helping others less experienced than you.

Remember this and you will feel better about asking for help. Approach a more experienced person in your sector – ask them how they got through the problems you may be experiencing now. Do this in the knowledge that one day you will be helping someone out who is in your shoes now.

"You must stay out there to let people know who you are and what you are doing," one Corporate Crossover told me. "Don't ever forget the little guy as you were once there and can be there again in a heartbeat. You get what you give."

Chapter 12: Don't cancel the cleaner

Scaling your business, creating systems and a sustainable revenue model that doesn't depend on you or your presence is essential for growth. If you want to grow your business and move beyond having an income to being financially free, you will have to ask for help. Whether the help is additional resources, advice or funding, it is important to resist getting to breaking point before you reach out.

Many of the women business owners I know find it difficult to ask for help. They need to get to bursting point before they make a request. This time is often too late.

There are studies that show that women are less likely to ask for help – we have been socialised to place the needs of others first. We expect to have to 'do it all' – often at great cost to our health and the potential of the business.

> "Women always try and make things perfect so the way we run a business also has to be perfect," says Joanne Napier. Her company, Linen Loft, uses mums as 'at-home' saleswomen, giving them the chance to work flexible hours. "There is no such thing as a perfect business. Things do fall off the side and some nights my kids do have readymade meals and I don't beat myself up about it. You can't do everything. In terms of business you have to do the best you can. Women are worse than men. My husband will make time to go to the gym every day because he needs to get fit – that's how he sees it. Women don't do that, but we also give ourselves such a hard time about making sure everything's right. I think we need to lighten up."

Break the cycle. You need to put your needs and the needs of your business first so that you can manage it optimally. If you as the business owner are tired, stressed, fed up and not doing the work that needs to be done, then your business will never reach those lofty heights you dreamed of at the start of your journey.

13 Is it worth it?

What women love about having their own businesses

My research found that 68% of the 300 business owners I surveyed were earning less than when they had a job. Yet two-thirds of these women said that even if they were offered a job with more money, they wouldn't return. They prefer running their own business and earning less money to a bigger income working as an employee.

It seems counterintuitive. Why would they prefer a pay cut and the stress of being a business owner to the ease and extra income of a job? The loss of income was more than compensated for by the satisfaction of running their own businesses.

Here are some of the reasons they gave me:

Flexibility

"I love the freedom to manage in my own style, the lack of corporate red tape, and always working towards a clear vision I create." That comment was typical of the answers I got when I asked these women why they loved their jobs. They love creating a direction, working out how to get there, and then making it happen. The knowledge that they are totally responsible for any outcome fuels them to greater achievements.

> Flexibility can mean not only working on what you want, but also working when you want. Zoe Sinclair: "I love that I'm doing something right, clients want me and clients keep coming back to me. But I think that the balance between my work and that I'm now home for my children every day is what I really love."

Freedom

Total freedom is compelling. One survey respondent comments: "I love the freedom to make my own decisions, the flexibility to work when I want as I work from home. I love the sense of achievement in starting my own business and making it successful. My confidence has grown hugely; I am inspired and motivated every day – which is a great feeling."

The successful women I spoke to loved having the freedom to do it all, to implement their own ideas, choose the type of employees they wanted and the clients they had. To create the culture they want to work in feeds them. It feeds their passion and they love it. The freedom of working how and when they want liberates them to make it feel as if it isn't work.

Being totally responsible for the result

It seems that the women who step out are ready to be completely accountable and responsible for their actions. The change from corporate life to self-employment is empowering. Running your own company gives you a clear sense of why things happen and makes you responsible for all the decisions and their outcomes. Observing your direct impact on a customer, on your marketing and on your business is very motivating and compelling.

"I love feeling inspired every day to make my business the best it can possibly be for my clients and customers," says one Corporate Crossover. "I didn't always respect the bosses I had in the corporate world, and I was disconnected from our actual customers and how they felt about the products."

Driving the business

By making all the decisions and setting the pace, you are able to drive the business in the direction you want it to go – and the rewards are all yours.

"I often didn't understand why certain decisions were made in the company and why I had to work so hard toward those goals. Even though I loved what I was working on, I felt like I was working every day to pay for our executives' luxury cars and mansions in other cities. In my own business, I'm working directly for the people I care most about. If we're changing something, it is because direct customer feedback told us to do so. I treat my customers as my managers – they decide where my priorities lie – and it always makes sense to me."

Moving at a faster pace

How much corporate workplace time is dedicated to actively making your work environment function, instead of actually just doing the work? How much time and energy is spent on scene-setting, lobbying, politics, approval seeking, presentations, stakeholder management, meetings and makeovers... Instead of just doing the work?

The liberation from all of the mechanics surrounding the work allows you to get more done and thus actually love what you do again. You can enjoy doing the work instead of being caught up and concerned about how you get it done. You know that there won't be any overturned decisions, political fall-out or second-guessing.

No wonder it doesn't feel like work anymore because it is pure and focused – and you know the exact purpose of the work at hand. It is for a real reason, not some political manoeuvring. Your energy and thinking is focused on the output, nothing else. You are single-minded: liberation, clarity and efficiency!

> Lucy Brazier says, "If I do something and it isn't working, I just cut it and do something different. I don't have to go through huge amounts of red tape and loads and loads of meetings to have somebody say, 'Yes, it's okay for you to change what you're doing'."
>
> After eleven years of working for a national retailer, Sally Preston was frustrated at the processes and feeling like an invisible component in a large machine. She loved having her own business: "From the start I found it liberating. I made all the decisions and moved at my very quick pace. It was fast moving with no committees and watering down of ideas. I loved the autonomy and being able to make things happen quickly.

Creativity

Without all the extra demands on your time, emotions and energy, you can let your creativity have free rein. Whether or not you run a 'creative' business, the process of creating something from nothing and of nurturing and feeding it to grow is enormously satisfying.

Julie Anixter, Co-Founder and Executive Editor at Innovation Excellence comments: "The reason that I left corporate America was that I wanted to be able to be more creative and faster in creating impact. I left so that I could fully operationalise, and fully express my vision. I would take any day being an accountable entrepreneur versus being an employee in an environment where there is overwhelming resistance to change, innovation and finding new solutions."

Freedom from the confines of the corporation also allows us to grow and learn in the way we choose. We have more energy left over to think expansively and creatively.

Being true to your values

Having your own business can also allow you to live by your own values and be true to yourself. The toxic environment at some corporate jobs can leave you feeling as though you are forced to work by the values of the company, even if they don't match your own.

Galia Orme of CHOC Chick was one of the many women who told me that this was one of the most rewarding aspects of being a business owner.

"I really love what I do. I'm very ethical and I really wanted to do things in a socially and environmentally conscious way. I'm able to do something that I really enjoy and achieve things in a manner that I'm very proud of." And Galia is walking the talk. By only sourcing free trade and ethically produced raw ingredients from South America, she knows her values reduce her profit margins. But she wouldn't have it any other way.

Chapter 13: Is it worth it?

As another survey respondent puts it, "If I'm going to work up to seventy hours a week I'd rather be doing it for myself instead of someone else. That way I can ensure that my own business values of authenticity and integrity are honoured."

Being around for the family

Leaving their corporate job to have more flexibility and spend more time with family is a key driver for a number of the women that responded to my survey. Starting and running your own business is all-consuming, so have these Corporate Crossovers designed the life they want?

> "I like to be there for my family," says Susan Moore, founder of Moore Virtual Assistance. "I had one morning when both my kids broke bones at school. I would have felt terrible sending a nanny or au pair to sort it out. And that's when you think, it's worth it. That you can take time out and you know if you do that, then you just put the hours back by working in the evening."

Loving it every day!

What about me? A decade on from being an unwilling Corporate Crossover, would I ever go back? It's highly unlikely. I know the toxic culture eroded a core part of me and my coping strategies were undeveloped. But it's more than that... I love my work. My heart sings when I work with a client to enable them to realise their goal, or bring them one step closer to their dream. I love the energy of leading workshops and liberating business ideas into the world. And most of all, I love the freedom to be me.

14 Bringing it all together

So you have decided that you want to crossover. Yes!

I'm delighted that you want to take the step and create your own business and take control of your life. Reading this book is a great foundation for the start of your journey to cross over but you also need a plan.

From my own experience and that of my clients, I know that as a Corporate Crossover, you will move through three phases on your journey – from the seed of an idea to actually starting your own business.

Phase 1: Clarity

First you need clarity – in your ideas and the reasons why you are starting the business.

Phase 2: Confidence

Then you need confidence. Confidence that your idea will work and that you have the skills and experience to make it a success.

Phase 3: Commitment

Finally, commitment. To create the business plan to bring your idea to life. To resign and start your new life!

Clarity

It is essential that you are clear about what you will be doing in your business and why you are doing it before you leave your job. Being clear about what you will be selling and who will be buying your product or service is a key foundation for any business start-up.

Often when you are thinking about starting your business, you may have many ideas, or be very imprecise about your idea. When you struggle to articulate your idea clearly, you will also find it hard to move forward. Until you know exactly what you are selling, and who to, it is difficult to generate momentum to work through the planning process.

Having clarity before you leave your job and creating artifacts (like your vision board) about what your new business and life will be like will assist you in times of doubt. In those times, you can forget why you thought this was such a great decision, and lose sight of the vision you had for the business and your new life. Having physical reminders of your initial enthusiasm and dream enables you to reconnect with the optimism and energy you had when you were starting out.

Activity to gain clarity:

1. **Develop a five-year vision for the business**
   - Create your vision board
   - Describe what this business will be like in five years' time

2. **Why do you want to do it?**
   - Dig deep about all the reasons why you want to leave your job and set up your business
   - Is it about leaving a legacy, financial, lifestyle or something else?

3. **What will you be selling?**
   - Write down what you will be selling, whether it be a product or service

- This is your chance to get all of your great ideas out of your head and onto paper!

4. **Who will buy it?**
   - Imagine who your ideal customer is
   - Create a profile of them, where they live, what they do, habits, lifestyle, etc.
   - How are their problems related to your business idea?

5. **Why would they buy your offering?**
   - Thinking about your idea, and their problems, how will your idea help your ideal customer?
   - What solutions are you offering?

These five steps will give you more clarity on your idea, and give you the impetus to move on to the next phase.

Confidence

Once you have clarity about the business you want to create and what you are selling, you need to have confidence that the business will be successful. This is the time to further define your offering and consider how you will stand out in the market. This means that you will need to start researching the market you wish to enter, the competition, and how you compare. At this stage you also need to be confident that you have the right mix of skills and experience for your business to be a success.

Activity to gain confidence:

1. **Understand the market space you will be entering**
   - Is the market growing or shrinking?
   - How big is it?
   - What are the key trends?

2. **Competition**
   - Who are your competitors in the market?
   - How do they compare to you?
   - What does your ideal customer love about them?

3. **Competitive advantage**
   - What does your competition do poorly?
   - How are they all priced?
   - How will you be better than your competition?

4. **Testing your idea**
   - Start to research about your idea against your ideal customer
   - Take on board their feedback and refine

5. **What skills do you need and what do you have already**
   - List all of the skills you may need to run your new business successfully
   - If you don't know what you may need, ask others in similar businesses
   - Then compare that list with the skills you currently have
   - Decide if you will acquire new skills or outsource

By completing these five steps, your confidence will grow about the feasibility of your idea. The more market information you acquire, the more knowledgeable you will be about what opportunities exist in this space.

Commitment

Now, with clarity and confidence in your business idea and your ability to do it, it is time to make the commitment.

You need to start the business planning process so you can gauge what is required, make your first sale, and then make a profit. Here you will investigate how much it will cost you to create your offering, the best way to reach your prospects, and then estimate your sales for year one.

This will start to give you a much greater degree of confidence and increase your commitment to crossing over.

If you are going to leave your job for this new venture, a little preparation and forethought will go a long way. As one Corporate Crossover commented: "I put a lot of thought into the decision to leave and thrashed it out a lot, but was nowhere near as thorough with the plan for building the business so it's been a real learning curve!" You can make this learning curve easier by taking the time to create a business plan.

Below is a simple structure for a business plan. This may be useful for you to get your idea out of your head and onto paper. If you think you will require funding and need a more extensive business plan and financials, then this will be a great place to capture your initial thinking before you start that larger planning process.

For more detailed information on creating Business Plans, including information, resources, worksheets and templates; then please see my second book: **"My New Business; a Busy Woman's Guide to Start-up Success."** This will be published in October 2014 by Pearson Education.

The key to remember with business plans is that one size will not fit all. If you are going to be setting up a large enterprise requiring premises, staff, an initial stock holding and funding, your business plan will be very different from someone who has decided to do what she does now but as a freelance consultant. In this case her capital requirements will be minimal and it is most likely that she will not be looking for funding.

Chapter 14: Bringing it all together

Activity for commitment: Creating a business plan

1. **Market analysis**
   - How big your market is, key trends, opportunities for future growth

2. **Vision**
   - Where do you want your business to be in five years' time?

3. **Value proposition**
   - What you are selling?
   - Who is your ideal client?
   - What problem are you solving?
   - Why would they buy your idea over the competition?
   - Why would they come back for more?

4. **Supporting market research findings**
   - Feedback on your idea from your ideal prospects

5. **Competitive analysis**
   - Who else is in your market space?
   - What makes them great and what could you do better?
   - Analyse their value proposition
   - Pricing analysis

6. **Year 1 goals**
   - What do you want to achieve in your first year?
   - Consider revenue, profit, operating expenses, number of customers, products launched

7. **SWOT and key focus areas**

- When you are considering achieving your goals, what are the Strengths, Weaknesses, Opportunities and Threats that will inhibit or support you?

- Once you have your SWOT, then devise your key focus areas for the business

8. **Bringing your idea to life – Production plan**

- How will you make or create your product or service?

- Sourcing suppliers, manufacturers

- Develop costs and timeframes

9. **Paths to market**

- Determine the best way to reach your ideal prospects (online, retail, wholesale, distributors)

- Establish relationships, fees and requirements expected

- Develop pathway to first sale

10. **Marketing plan**

- Branding – What will you name your business or product?

- How will you attract prospects and convert them to paying customers?

- What marketing activity will you do – and when?

- How much do you plan to spend?

11. **Operations plan**

- Decide business entity

- Detail of your business infrastructure

- Communications, staff, premises, business systems

- Estimates of initial and on-going costs for operations

12. The numbers

- Creation of a profit and loss statement; detail expected revenue, estimated outgoings to forecast profit or loss
- Estimate of cash inflows and outflows based on forecast production and sales
- Funding requirements and options

13. Why this will succeed

- What skills and experience do you and your team (if you have one) bring to the business?
- What market opportunity, or changing consumer trend, are your seizing?
- Bring your ideas together to convince someone to support you!

What are you waiting for?

If you're not yet ready to quit your job, don't let that stop you from taking the first steps toward starting your business. You can achieve a surprising amount while you are still employed.

Many of the small administrative jobs that need to be completed to start a company are quick and easy to do. A few have waiting times – and why not do that waiting while you're still earning a paycheck? Use your free time at work, evenings and weekends to start crossing over.

1. Write your business plan

Take the time to plan your business – both the 'back of an envelope' plan and a more detailed version as outlined above. A business plan helps you spot any potential problems with your business model. It will help you explain your business to other people, and you can show it to lenders when you're looking for finance. Business plans also improve performance –

studies indicate that businesses which plan regularly make higher profit margins compared with businesses that don't do regular planning.

2. **Survey people you know about whether they think they would buy what you are selling**

   Not all business ideas are good ones, unfortunately. Even if you do have all the drive an entrepreneur needs, some ideas will not succeed. If your business idea is weak and there is no demand for your product or service, it's best to find out before you've quit your job and sunk your time and money into a start-up. Simply start by sending an email to supportive friends and family members and see what kind of response you get.

3. **Research company structures**

   Will you be a sole trader? Is your business going to be a partnership? Or will a standard company structure work best for you? Your local government website will include information about the pros and cons of each type of company structure. You need to consider the future of your business – you may be a sole trader now, but do you plan to take on staff members in the future? You also need to think about the tax implications of each structure; talk to an accountant about which structure would suit you best.

4. **Create a business name**

   If a name for your new business, product or service hasn't already leapt out at you, don't panic. Start to keep a list of ideas you like and then make a shortlist to research. Try to choose a name that is easy to spell and that your clients will understand. If it is also different and memorable, even better!

   With your shortlist, start to search on Google or at Companies House if the name is available for a business entity. Search to see what domain names are available.

Chapter 14: Bringing it all together

5. Which domain names could you use?

Even if you pick a fantastic name, it's not going to be a good choice if you can't use it on your website. Look for a domain name which will work with your company name and buy it as soon as you can.

6. Register your company name

You do this online with your national company register: it takes only a few minutes and once it's done you're officially a business director.

7. Get a tax number

Once your company is registered, you need to register it with the tax office. This is in most cases another five-minute job.

8. Open a bank account for your business

Armed with your official company registration details and your tax number, you can open a bank account for your business. This means you are ready to start billing immediately.

9. Plan the website

For most types of business, your website needs to be up and running as soon as, or even before, you get your first customer. It's your business card to the world, and it should reflect all your plans for your company. It doesn't have to be expensive; a basic Wordpress site can work for most small businesses and can be linked to your domain name at a very reasonable price.

10. Plan for funding

How are you going to fund the business before you make the first sale? Will there be a shortfall – how long will it last and how will you cover it? Once you know the numbers, you can make a push to secure financing. It could be from venture capitalists, angel investors, the bank, or friends and family. Start thinking about where that money will come from, how you will secure it, and when you will be able to pay it back.

11. Create a sample product

If you're selling a product, create a sample and do some testing on friends. If you're selling a service, think about how you can create a 'sample' – it could be a portfolio of work you've done in the past, or a collection of testimonials from some of your biggest clients.

12. Research your competitors

Who are you going to be competing against in the marketplace? Which companies do you want to emulate? Spend some time online looking at the ways that brands you like set themselves apart. Look for a niche where you can position your company. Also investigate your competitors' pricing – where will yours sit in comparison?

13. Set up social media accounts

If you're planning to use social media, set up accounts now so they're ready for business as soon as you are. Start to connect with opinion leaders in your market, and observe what is being communicated.

These tasks are all essential to the formation of a business so, with these completed, you are well on your way to having the basic business administration under control. Each type of business will also have other details to attend to – it could be setting up an e-commerce site, getting barcodes, international tax numbers or import/export accounts. Try to identify if you can do any of these before you finish your full-time job, particularly if they involve delays that will prevent you from trading.

Does this seem prosaic and dull? I'm afraid there is no getting around it – running your own business involves not only excitement and enthusiasm but also routine administration and accounting. That's why you need to have so much passion and commitment to your ideas. That way you can keep your eye on the dream when you feel you are down in the details.

The end is the beginning for you

Eleven years on and three country moves later, my business keeps evolving and thriving as I do. It has given me the opportunity to fulfill a lifelong dream of travelling through Europe and the US for six months while still working. I have now created a completely location independent business and I love it. It has supported my family as sole breadwinner for eight years, and provided a welcome respite for me from grief, family illness and despair.

Through my business I have made lifelong friends around the world and continue to be stretched, challenged and stimulated. I can be as creative as I choose and design my time to suit what I want.

I have complete freedom and flexibility.

Often when we think of making a change we hold on to what we are leaving behind instead of eagerly anticipating where we are going. If this sounds like you, start to shift your thinking about possibility and opportunity.

Becoming a Corporate Crossover has worked for me, and for thousands of other women. If you are thinking of leaving your job, take the steps to make it real.

Work through the exercises in this book, create a plan to get clarity and confidence about your idea and the viability of it. Then take the next step and write the business plan. Not a stuffy one hundred page document you create once and never revisit, but a plan you will love and use as your roadmap.

When you are ready to take this step, read my next book: **"A Busy Woman's Guide to Starting Her Business"**. This is to be published by Pearson in October 2014.

I wish you all the best as you start your journey. I would love to know where you are at, your successes, your low points and everything in between! Do drop me a line at wendy@corporatecrossovers.com or connect with me on Linked In or twitter @Wendy_kerr

And don't forget to download the exercises and worksheets at www.corporatecrossovers.com/when-its-time.

About the Author

Wendy Kerr is passionate about changing the way work works. She is on a mission to fuel 10,000 women to create a business that allows them to live the life they love.

With a 20-year career in multi-national blue chip organisations, she has specialised in creating and launching new businesses around the world. Her business experience includes:

- Starting a digital content business in London, expanding it globally and acquiring three media companies,

- As General Manager of FT.com personal finance, leading the business and team through the dot com crash, restructuring it for profitability

- Starting an online share trading site in Australia and listing it on the Australian stock exchange, raising $70 million at the start of the first dot com boom in the '90s

A Corporate Crossover herself, Wendy left her corporate career to create a successful six-figure coaching and consulting business, running it from London and Tokyo. She works with leaders of high growth, global technology companies in challenging times of expansion and change. Client companies include Expedia, IBM, ACCA, The Economist and Betfair.

Wanting to change the way work works, she has also coached, mentored and fuelled over 1,500 women to create a business that allows them to live the life they love.

Her company, Corporate Crossovers®, enables women wherever they are in their journey of leaving their job to start their business successfully, providing them with structure, tools, processes and one on one mentoring.

She leads a vibrant and dynamic community of Corporate Crossovers® around the world who are focused on creating the life they want, providing even more support, ideas and advice for the journey.

Being true to her mission of enabling women to create businesses to support the life they love, she recently fulfilled a long held dream of living in the South of France and travelling through Europe and the US in an RV with her family, all while running her six-figure business remotely.

A frequent media commentator, Wendy was interviewed on BBC Radio 4 Women's Hour discussing her research on how women are changing the way work works. She was featured in The Japan Times discussing the role of coaching in life and career transition. Wendy also writes regularly for The Guardian (UK), The Business (Sweden) and Women Unlimited Worldwide on how to create a business to live the life you love.

She can be found at www.Corporatecrossovers.com, Linked In, Facebook, G+ and on twitter at @wendy_kerr

Acknowledgements

Leaving your job to start your own business is a journey. Writing a book about it has involved a physical journey for me and my family, spanning two years and living in three countries, and travelling extensively around the US in an RV.

To the many Corporate Crossovers I interviewed for this book, thank you for taking the time to speak with me, review comments and support me in this quest – thank you so much, as I know how precious your time is. Each time I read your words, I get re-inspired, so I know you will touch the readers too.

Like any great endeavour, many people have helped me bring it to life. Firstly my wonderful coach Laura West, who inspired and created the name Corporate Crossovers, and encouraged me to write a book.

My dear friend Emma, who even going through her own personal journey, provided her 16th Century barn in beautiful Hampshire as my author's retreat.

Betsy Rapoport gave me generous advice that transformed the book's structure, and inspired confidence to let my voice come though after reviewing my first draft. To my editor, Amy Hamilton-Chadwick who tightened up my prose and enabled me to keep on track with the writing.

As I have discovered, writing the book is only half the work. Launching and marketing the book, is just as essential. Jacqueline Biggs, another great coach of mine, has given me the oomph and strategy to ensure my book reaches as many people as possible.

Mike for not letting me give up on this project. And to my darlings,

Ant and Liberty, for being so understanding when the book writing came before their games of Lego, reading, cards and playing in the sun.

To my siblings and their partners - thank for your unwavering support and inspiration as you continue to build your businesses.

And to anyone who is thinking of crossing over, or has already done it – thanks for reading the book, and I wish you vibrant success in your ventures!

Please, do drop me a line and tell me of your journey,

Warmly,

Wendy

wendy@corporatecrossovers.com
www.CorporateCrossovers.com

Thanks to Xero for their support in enabling Corporate Crossovers to learn to love their numbers!

Connect with Wendy

Email: wendy@corporatecrossovers.com

Web: www.corporatecrossovers.com

Twitter: @wendy_kerr

Linked In: uk.linkedin.com/in/wendyrkerr/

Google +: +WendyKerr

Facebook Page: www.facebook.com/CorporateCrossovers

Facebook: www.facebook.com/wendyrkerr

Coming soon

*My New Business; a Busy Woman's Guide
to Start-up Success*

October 2014

www.ingramcontent.com/pod-product-compliance
Lightning Source LLC
Chambersburg PA
CBHW071546200326
41519CB00021BB/6627